THE
NOVEL
WRITER'S
BLUEPRINT

THE NOVEL WRITER'S BLUEPRINT

FIVE STEPS TO CREATING AND COMPLETING YOUR FIRST BOOK

DEVELOPED BY KEVIN T. JOHNS

AUTHOR OF THE PAGE TURNERS

CAT & BEAN PUBLISHING

OTTAWA, ONTARIO, CANADA

Special discounts are available on quantity purchases. For details, contact the copyright holder at kevintjohns@gmail.com.

First Edition (print and electronic), 2014.

The Novel Writer's Blueprint: Five Steps to Creating and Completing Your First Book / Kevin T. Johns — 1st ed.
ISBN 978-0-9920041-2-5 (paperback)
ISBN 978-0-9920041-3-2 (electronic)

Printed and bound in the United States of America,
by CreateSpace, an Amazon Company.

The cover of this book is acid-free; the pages are acid-free and lignin-free; both the cover and the pages meet all of the American National Standards Institute's criteria for archival-quality paper.

Set in **Dante Monotype Standard**, **Chunk**, and **Futura**. Author photograph: **Melanie Shields** (*melanieshieldsphotography.com*). Novel Writer's Blueprint logo: original by **Kit Foster** (*kitfosterdesign.com*). Editing, diagrams, interior design, diagrams, cover design, and logo revision: **Forrest Adam Sumner** (*brillianteditions.com*).

www.yournovelblueprint.com

*For every teacher
with the generosity
to share*

*And every student
with the humility
to learn.*

Contents

Preface

This book was developed simultaneously with the on-line course of the same name, and therefore features much of the same content.

Different students have different needs. Some people prefer to learn from the lectures and slides of an online course, while others favour the simplicity of a good, old-fashioned book (or ebook!).

Those in a third group, in which I count myself, prefer to experience the same content several times, in order to ensure maximum absorption. I thoroughly enjoyed Tim Grahl's CreativeLive course *Sell Your First 1000 Books*; but afterwards I still purchased and read *Your First 1000 Copies*, Grahl's book containing the same content. By confronting the information twice, in two formats, I was able to digest the content all the better.

That's why I've produced a variety of formats to help writers learn from the NOVEL WRITER'S BLUEPRINT program. If you love learning independently with a book in your hand, then I hope you will enjoy this written version of the course.

If you're curious about what the online experience entails, I encourage you to visit *yournovelblueprint.com*. In addition to the course's video modules, the online version of THE NOVEL WRITER'S BLUEPRINT includes a great deal of bonus material that can help you to create and complete your first novel.

Once your manuscript is drafted and ready for professional editing, I encourage you to visit my editor, Forrest Adam Sumner, at *brillianteditions.com* for all your editing and layout needs.

Finally, if you are interested in reading my novels, which illustrate several examples throughout this book, please, visit *thepageturnerstrilogy.com*, where you can download ebooks instantly and have paperbacks delivered to your door.

THE NOVEL WRITER'S BLUEPRINT

Introduction

It took me eight gruelling years to write and publish my first novel . . . and about two months to write the sequel.

In the guidebook you're now reading, I'm going to walk you through exactly the same system that I developed and implemented to accomplish that feat, the system that allowed me to do in eight weeks what first had taken me eight years. Now *you* will be able to write *your* novel with speed and efficiency.

Getting Lost in the Void

But, before we get into the nuts and bolts of the program and begin working on your novel, I want you to take a moment to contemplate something that most writers find terrifying. Ready for it? Brace yourself. Here it comes:

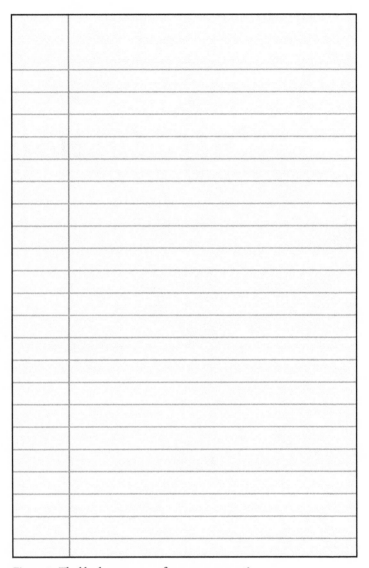

Figure 1. The blank page—your fearsome opponent?

That's right—the blank page. For all but a handful of writers, there's nothing scarier than having to sit down and conquer the empty computer screen or clean sheet of paper. It lies there, pristine as freshly fallen snow, taunting you, daring you to sully it with your stilted prose and awkward narratives. It's terrifying.

Some people call this fear *writer's block*. I call it *getting lost in the void*. But, regardless of what we name this evil behemoth, there's no denying that the fear that it instills can be a major deterrent to the creative process.

It's no wonder that so many people have such a difficult time writing their first book!

But I want to tell you something: the blank screen need not bring you existential angst. I'll tell you why, and you might find my answer a little bit controversial; but, by the end of this book, I promise you, you'll agree with me.

You don't need to fear the blank screen because . . . *there is no such thing as writer's block!*

There are only writers who aren't willing to do the planning and the training necessary before diving in to writing their manuscript, and who haven't developed the skills to keep going and stay on track once they've started writing.

That feeling of writer's block, of being lost in the void and overwhelmed, is something *you* never need feel again.

You now have a blueprint to follow.

Streamlining

So, back to that question. If writing my first novel took me eight years, how did my second book, of comparable length, take just eight weeks?

Well, I read a really important book—*The 4-Hour Chef*, by Tim Ferriss. If you haven't read it already, I highly recommend that you check it out. Ostensibly, it's a book that teaches you how to cook; but, in fact, it just uses cooking as an example of how to learn any new skill. To put it another way, it's a book about learning that just happens to teach you how to cook.

Early in the book, Ferriss outlines what he calls **DiSS**, the method that he uses when learning a new skill. "DiSS" stands for "Deconstruction, Selection, Sequencing, and Stakes".

When it came time for me to write the sequel to *The Page Turners*, I was not willing to spend another eight years writing, as I'd done on the first book. Having just read *The 4-Hour Chef*, I decided to apply the DiSS method to my writing and see where it led me.

I *deconstructed* the process I went through to finish that first novel. I *selected* the key steps that helped me to succeed; and I pruned out those steps that didn't work, held me back, and stood in my way. All the challenges that I faced, and mistakes that I made early on and had to go back and fix later, were removed from my workflow, until all I had left was a handful of steps for success. I then *sequenced* those steps so that each one built on the one before. Finally, I established *stakes* that kept me on track by spelling out negative consequences for losing my way during the novel-writing process.

Suddenly, producing a novel was no longer a humongous, all-encompassing, overwhelming project. Instead, it was a logical, simple, step-by-step process, the very system outlined in the book now in your hands—THE NOVEL WRITER'S BLUEPRINT: FIVE STEPS TO CREATING AND COMPLETING YOUR FIRST BOOK.

This book includes this introductory section and a concluding chapter; but the core of the program consists of five simple steps:

1. **Genre Selection.** Genre isn't where most people begin, but it's a super-helpful way to start developing your narrative—especially if you're a first-time novelist.

2. **Story Structure.** Here we'll identify the structures that have developed over the history of storytelling and have proven successful with readers time and time again. You'll use the power of those structures to organize your thinking and plotting during the development of your novel.

3. **Puzzle Work.** This innovative technique is where we'll look at specific scenes and memorable passages that you'd like to create or emulate, and then you'll use them to begin piecing your story together.

4. **Preparatory Regimen.** We'll examine how to get yourself into shape for the novel-writing endeavor.

5. **Running the Marathon.** This is where we get into the actual drafting process. It's a marathon, people!

I'm not going to tell you that writing a novel is easy. It's not. Even with this book to help you, it will be hard work.

But I *know* you can do it.

You've taken the time to find this book, you've spent your hard-earned money to purchase it, and you've read this far. That means that you have the dedication and passion necessary to make it happen.

You just need a system.

What the Blueprint Covers

When you're taking a course or reading an instructional book, it's important to remind yourself of what you hope to get from the content—so let's take a moment to identify this book's goals.

By the end of THE NOVEL WRITER'S BLUEPRINT, you will have learned so much:

- How to overcome writer's block *forever*
- Why *formula* does not mean *formulaic*
- How to harness the power of genre
- The importance of emulating successful artists and mentors
- The story structures that are best to build *your* narrative
- How the scientific method can be applied to writing
- Why developing an idea, concept, or premise is *not* where you want to begin
- How to develop your novel's key scenes and complete what I call the **puzzle work**
- Techniques that will help you overcome the four major challenges that authors face while writing
- The role that community plays in producing a novel
- How to lay the groundwork for success by imple-

menting a preparatory regimen
- The value of tools and systems that keep you accountable and on track
- How to use nine different creative exercises to sharpen your skills
- The secret trick that successful novelists use to find the time to write each day
- How to identify dozens of real-world examples of these principles in action, from novels, films, and television.

Pneumonia Angels, or Why Art Matters

I want to tell you a story about pneumonia angels.

About a year ago, I caught pneumonia. Things weren't going too well for me, and the stress took such a toll on me physically that I fell seriously ill.

If you've ever had pneumonia, you know it is pretty darn bad. You can see why people die from it. You can barely breathe, you can barely *move*, and it lasts for weeks.

I was lying on my couch with this pneumonia, feeling pretty down, feeling as if I were going to die, and thinking that dying might not be the worst thing that could happen to me. Doped up on antibiotics and other drugs the doctors put me on, I was just flipping through the channels, staring at the television—but not actually watching anything.

I ended up on Ellen DeGeneres's talk show right as this band, Tegan and Sara, was beginning to perform a song. For some reason—I can't explain it exactly—it was one of those performances that touched my soul.

I fell in love with Tegan and Sara. In the weeks that followed, I obsessed over their catalogue of albums; but, before that, in that initial moment of total despair and dire illness, they appeared to me as angels. It was as if they were metaphysical messengers from God, sent to tell me there was a reason to get better, that I could pull through the sickness and get back on my feet, and that my life could turn around for the better.

Ever since then, I have thought of Tegan and Sara as my pneumonia angels.

Why am I telling you this story?

What on earth do pneumonia angels have to do with writing a novel?

Well, I bring all this up to emphasize a point: *Art saves lives.* Tegan and Sara's song—that unique combination of lyrics, melody, and performance—spoke to me in such a personal way, and called forth from within me such a profound sense of joy, that it made me want to go on living. From the depths of life's bitter well, from beneath the ugly countenance of sickness and failure that I saw everywhere I looked at that moment in my life, I caught a glimpse of something beautiful flowing out of the television and across the living room to where I lay on the couch. It touched my flesh, filled my wheezing lungs, and permeated my consciousness. In doing so, the song reminded me of the elations that make life worth living, and of the bliss that is worth striving, through all of the strife, to achieve.

The crafting of a novel, the creation of any work of art, is a battle between the forces of life and the forces of death. There is something creative within all of us, and it is our duty to our fellow human beings to get that something *out* before death claims us.

This isn't just a hobby you're starting on here. You're not just creating escapism for your readers. Yes, it is a hobby, and it is escapism. But it's also so much more: we're talking about a real battle between life and death, between creation and destruction.

Making art is immeasurably important.

Art, when we create it and especially when we take it in, is what keeps us going through our darkest days. Art is what we turn to for aid in our most desperate hour. Art is what shows us why life is worth living, despite the despair threatening to crush us into dust. As you read through this book and as you engage in your own writing, I want you to keep that always in mind.

Consider the following quote from the film *Point Break* for a moment. The movie isn't very highly regarded, and it is a bit silly; but there is some great pedigree behind its scenes—it was directed by Kathryn Bigelow, the first woman to win an Oscar for Best Director, and the executive producer was James Cameron.

In the film, a team of bank robbers, who also happen to be passionate surfers and thrill-seekers, discuss why they do what they do. Their leader offers this explanation:

> " *This was never about money for us. It was about us against the system—that system that kills the human spirit. We stand for something. To those dead souls inching along the freeways in their metal coffins—we show them that the human spirit is still alive.* "

These are the lines of a fictional character talking about why he and his friends rob banks, but I think it's fairly easy to argue that this is also Kathryn Bigelow and James Cameron explaining to the audience why it is that they create art.

Another great quote that I often come back to is from Kurt Vonnegut's book *Timequake*:

> " *I say in speeches that a plausible mission of artists is to make people appreciate being alive at least a little bit. I am then asked if I know of any artists who pulled that off. I reply, 'The Beatles did.'* "

You bet The Beatles did! And so did Kurt Vonnegut.

These artists are the authors of our culture, and the books and music they create are the language with which we weave our cultural narratives.

Whether you think the society you live in is perfect or not, you have a duty to contribute your unique perspective to the cultural discourse. If you want the world to change for the better, you need to write about how it could be better. Or, if you like it the way it is and you think its current state needs to be protected and cherished, you need to write about *that*.

As a novelist, you must never forget that you aren't just a writer: you're an author of your culture. And, by this, I don't just mean that you are an author who *is shaped by* that culture: I also mean that *you shape your culture*.

It takes guts to define a culture. It's a big responsibility. By reading this book and by choosing to write a novel, you've taken that responsibility onto yourself.

It can be intimidating, but you must soldier forth.

Film, Books, and Why Now Is the Time to Take Action

I'm going to tell you a bit about my background—and, more important, discuss the unique moment in history that we are now experiencing in the book-publishing industry.

I fell in love with film after discovering an old edition of Gerald Mast's *A Short History of the Movies*, a book in my high-school library. It had this great cover, illustrated with images from *Annie Hall*, *Casablanca*, and *Lawrence of Arabia*—all films I had never seen at the time. The book introduced me to the idea of studying art from an academic perspective, and to the importance of understanding the *history* of an art form.

After high school, I began working in the film industry. The highlight of this period probably was getting to meet James Earl Jones, the voice of Darth Vader himself! I quickly learned, however, that making movies is largely construction work. It didn't take long for me to realize that my passion was for telling and studying stories, not lugging around lighting-equipment and reels of film stock. So, although I went to university to study film, I soon found myself falling in love with English literature, and I ended up getting my master's degree in that field, rather than film.

I mention this film background not just to help you understand where I am coming from as a writer and instructor, but also because you and I are going to look at examples from film throughout this book to illustrate and investigate concepts, even though our interest is how those concepts can help you in your novel-writing.

I've taken a lot of online courses and read many books on writing, and it used to irritate me a little when instructors and authors used examples from film, rather than literature. But, as I was putting together this book and the related online course material, I quickly realized why so many people draw from cinema for their examples: although we all have our own little niches that we're passionate about in the world of literature, Hollywood cinema is the common language that we *all* speak. I can't guarantee that you have read *A Farewell to Arms* and *The Great Gatsby*, but there is a pretty good chance you've seen *Star Wars* and *The Wizard of Oz*.

Anyway, after university, I thought I would kill some time before starting my doctorate studies, so I got a job with the federal government. For the first time in my life, I had money—and, before I knew it, I got engaged, I bought a house, and I had some kids. Suddenly I had a mortgage to pay, a family to support, a stable career—and getting that Ph.D. was *never* going to happen.

The problem was that my career didn't give me access to what I was most passionate about; I wasn't doing what I loved. My passion has always been for storytelling; and I knew I had a novel in me—just as I know you have a novel within *you*. They say the most valuable real-estate in any town is the graveyard, because it's full of businesses never launched and novels never written. I didn't want that to be my life story.

I worked for year after year on my debut novel, *The Page Turners*, writing and re-writing whenever I had spare time.

I made many mistakes, and learned many valuable lessons, over all those drafts and all those years.

Now, because it took me so long to write, something really interesting happened during the book's drafting: there was a major shift in the publishing industry. Thanks to print-on-demand and ebooks, getting the nod of approval from the industry's gatekeepers—those major publishing-houses who for so long had stood watch over the industry—was no longer a requirement. In addition, independent authors no longer had to order huge print runs of their self-published books, and now the up-front costs of publishing a book are lower than ever before.

In fact, these days, you can produce an ebook with virtually no investment whatsoever. I don't recommend it, and later I'll identify parts of the job where you *will* want to spend some money on your book's production. But the point is that it has never been easier to publish a book.

Writers no longer have the excuse that sending out query letters and dealing with endless rejections from agents and publishers is too much to handle. The real challenge now is getting that manuscript *written*. You no longer need to spend time on any of that interaction with the traditional behemoths in the publishing industry. Thanks to today's technology, you can concentrate your energy on writing the best books possible. That's why THE NOVEL WRITER'S BLUE-PRINT is almost singularly focused on getting you ready to *create* and *complete* your manuscript. *That* is the hard part.

Be a Doer

Shortly, we'll be diving in to the real meat of this book. But, before we do, I want to remind you that it's simply not good enough to be a learner and thinker: you have to be an implementer and a doer.

Remember—there is no such thing as a million-dollar idea, only a million-dollar *action*. Reading this book won't benefit you much if you never act on what you learn.

I don't expect you to take every single strategy discussed here and use it exactly as I have. I simply want you to take the elements that resonate with you, the ideas that you think will help you as an artist, and then put them to work for you. But you do have to take action.

You must! Do it for yourself; do it for your culture.

The Importance of Modelling

We human beings are storytellers. We always have been, going all the way back to 40,000-year-old cave paintings. (They're caveman comic books!) That means we can learn from tens of thousands of years of storytelling.

People, and artists in particular, love to think of the age in which they live as being of singular importance in human history; but the world did not start with you, my friend, and it won't end with you. I don't want to go all Project Mayhem and start yelling, "You are not special. You're not a beautiful and unique snowflake." You are, you are—everyone reading this book is a unique snowflake. But you're a snowflake that is part of the snowball that is human history rolling through time.

In 1623, John Donne wrote, in his *Devotions upon Emergent Occasions*, that "No man is an island entire of itself; every man is a piece of the continent, a part of the main." Donne's point was that we can't lock ourselves away and pretend we are not part of the larger world. And that world includes the history of writing that came before us. (Donne wrote that passage after a period of life-threatening illness, by the way; perhaps he had his own pneumonia angels!)

When you do ignore the larger world, you end up like Henry Darger, the subject of the documentary film *In the Realms of the Unreal*. He was essentially a shut-in—but one who wrote thousands of pages of fiction, and produced hundreds of drawings and paintings to illustrate his epic novel. The 15,145-page work was discovered only after Darger's death. His creation is extremely bizarre and undeniably unique, but I doubt it is the type of art you're looking to produce when you sit down to write your first novel.

I'm guessing you want to write something that connects with readers and moves as many people as possible. If you're going to do that, you need to acknowledge that you are part of something greater than yourself.

You've probably heard the saying "It's more of an art than a science" a million times. Asked how to score a goal in hockey, an athlete responds, "Well, it's more of an art than a science."

And what do we think of when we consider the artist figure in our society? We love this idea of the artist that originated with the Romantic poets, people such as Wordsworth, Coleridge, Shelley, and Byron: artists are these transcendent figures who sit alone in nature, waiting for inspiration, waiting for the muse to breathe the life of art into them.

Because this image of the romantic artist is so firmly ingrained in our minds, we don't flip the "more of an art than a science" concept on its head nearly often enough. You need to say to yourself, "Writing a novel is more of a science than an art!"

You must produce your writing consciously, actively—not simply hope that it flows out of you as a perfectly constructed story brought to you by some muse. If you buy in to the myth that Coleridge didn't know what he was doing when he wrote "Kubla Khan", that he was just high on opium and it was some purely metaphysical experience, then you've been misled by a couple hundred years of marketing-hype. I assure you that Coleridge knew what he was doing. You think a guy who wrote a book called *Biographia Literaria* didn't approach his art consciously?

How about another example? We can look to an even

more recent opium addict: Kurt Cobain. In the documentary *Kurt Cobain: About a Son*, you can hear just how conscious Cobain was of what he was doing. He talks about wanting to create music that had the emotion of heavy metal and the pop sensibilities of top-40 radio. He describes it as "Black Sabbath meets The Bay City Rollers", which is a pretty spot-on description of the music that his band, Nirvana, created. Cobain knew exactly what he was doing when he developed the music that inspired so many people of my generation.

Art and science do not exist independently of each other. There is an intimate relationship between the two. Scientists like Albert Einstein and Stephen Hawking have some of the most active and artistic imaginations possible, and artists like Kurt Cobain are often interested in aspects of the scientific world; you can see Cobain's interest in biology in the artwork on the cover of Nirvana's *In Utero* album.

Of course, when it comes to writing, there is also a third element, which mingles with art and science—and that is *magic*. Magic is that intangible element, that lightning in a bottle, that everyone wants but only a rare few succeed in capturing.

I would like to suggest, however, that magic is too often played up in novel-writing, and indeed in the arts in general. The result is that the nuts-and-bolts, scientific approach doesn't get the emphasis it deserves. This is unfortunate because, while the scientific method may not be sexy, it really works.

If, like me, you haven't taken a science course in about twenty years, here's a quick reminder of the steps involved in the scientific method:

1. **Observation.** I notice that water turns to ice during the winter.
2. **Hypothesis.** I suspect that it turns to ice when the temperature drops below zero degrees Celsius.
3. **Prediction.** I predict that if I put water in a freezer below zero, it will turn to ice.
4. **Experiment.** I put the water in the freezer.
5. **Conclusion.** I review the results and draw a conclusion: yup, that's ice alright!

The heart of the method is repeatable tests that prove (or disprove) a hypothesis, resulting in a conclusion. Believe it or not, even in something as seemingly unscientific as storytelling, hundreds of thousands of tests have shown us exactly what works. If you want to see the results of those experiments, all you have to do is visit your local library. Every one of those books is an experiment in form and content, and the books that have stood the test of time and are still being read today are the ones that have resonated best with readers. Their writers are the masters.

There is a saying that "Success leaves clues." The essential elements of effective storytelling aren't a mystery. You don't have to stare at that blank screen and hope that the answers will reveal themselves to you by magic. The answers are already out there for *you* to find. You just have to use the masters as your models—I call it **modelling the masters**. In doing so, you can stand on the shoulders of giants and use the formulas and blueprints for success that they have left behind for you.

I know some of you are thinking, "But, Kevin, I'm an *artist*! I want to follow my own path. I want to do something that's never been done before. I didn't get into novel-writing so that I could blindly follow some formula."

I hear you—but following a formula, learning from what has been successful in the past, does not produce formulaic art. This is because what differentiates your art from anyone else's art is the unique perspective that you bring to it.

Let's use three authors as an example: Chester Brown, Joe Matt, and Seth. All three artists work in autobiographical graphic novels. Each is both a writer and an illustrator. All three are former residents of Toronto. And, in fact, the three artists are good friends with one another—so, because they write autobiographical stories, they often appear in one another's work. You can read Joe Matt's *Spent* and see him talking with Brown and Seth. You can read Seth's *It's a Good Life if You Don't Weaken* and see him sitting at a diner with Chester Brown. You can read Brown's *Paying for It* and see him chatting with Matt and Seth.

These are three close friends, all telling stories that are in the same genre and set in the same town, featuring the same characters, using the same medium . . . and yet each of their books is vastly different from those of the others, and none of it feels formulaic in the slightest. Other than the shared surface elements, there's little similarity among the books of these three writers. This is because each one of them brings to his work such a singular perspective on the world.

As a student of literature, I'm asked, "How can you study literature? Hasn't everything that could possibly be written about Shakespeare already been written?" The answer is "No", because each one of us brings his or her own, unique viewpoint to a new reading of Elizabethan and Jacobean theatre and poetry. This is the core concept of something called *literary theory*.

Literary theory tells us that we can come away with vastly different readings of a text, and that these differences depend on what theoretical lens is applied to the reading. A Marxist reading of a text might focus on economic issues at play; a feminist reading would focus on issues of sex and gender; a structuralist approach—which, to an extent, we're going to take in this book—would try to identify the text's underlying archetypical story structures; a post-colonial analysis would bring a political perspective; and a national approach would examine how cultural issues of nationhood play out in the story.

You view the world through a specific lens, which gives you a unique perspective on the world. You therefore have no need to get experimental with the *formal elements*[1] of your work—especially in your first novel. Once you have a few books in the can and rabid fans who will buy whatever you put out, have at it. Until then, focus on the basic craft of your art form.

There's another reason to model the masters. I saw this quote on Facebook the other day: "I don't want my daughter to follow in my footsteps. I want her to walk alongside the path I've laid, and then go further than I ever could." Regardless of what you think about those words in relation to parenting, I think they can be applied quite helpfully to learning to write a novel. You, the new writer, are the child; and the masters are the parent. You cannot simply pick up where they left off and immediately take things further. First you must start where they started, walk the path they've laid, and learn the lessons that they've left along the way. Only then can you go further than they ever could.

When you think of paintings by Pablo Picasso, you may think of his famous Cubist work—but Picasso didn't start with Cubism. His earlier, pre-Cubist works, such as the paintings from his Blue Period, were remarkably realistic in comparison to what people generally think of as "a Pi-

---

[1]   These are the elements that make up the basic form.

casso". You need to learn the basic elements of your craft before you start pressing the boundaries. It's what Picasso did. It's what all the great artists and writers do.

And you do that by modelling. Modelling isn't an attempt at exact mimicry: it means emulating what the masters have done, while also bringing your own unique perspective to the work.

Homework

As you know, simply reading this book will not be enough for you to achieve your goal of writing a novel: you need to implement what you learn. To help you in turning these lessons into actions, the conclusion of each chapter in this book includes one or more homework assignments, and occasionally there are homework assignments at the ends of sections within chapters. I encourage you to complete this work before moving on to the next chapter. The more you give these assignments the attention they deserve, the more help they will give you in realizing your dream of writing and finishing your novel.

Your first assignment starts with this question: Who are your pneumonia angels? What do they bring to their art that inspires you and that you would like to emulate in your own work? Also, list at least five of your favourite scenes from novels, television, theatre, and/or movies; we'll return to this list later.

Step One: Genre Selection

If you know me and my work, you probably aren't all that surprised that genre is where I want to begin.

What Is Genre?

The term itself is a French word; it means a "kind" of something, or a "sort" of something. The idea of sorting art into categories is nothing new: it goes back to the Ancient Greeks. And the process is certainly not limited to literature: as human beings, we simply love categorizing and subcategorizing. In the context of this book, specifically, I want you to think of genre as a method for cataloguing and organizing story conventions.

With a project as massive as a novel, organization is key. It's one of the topics we're going to cover in great detail in this book, because you need to organize your ideas, story, and workflow to ensure that you're as efficient as possible in the drafting of your novel.

Another Meaning

In his review of my first book, critic Brendan Blom wrote, "Johns's crimson-stained love letter to genre fiction kept me reading late into the night." When I saw that, I got shivers! I'd never thought of my novel in those exact terms, but "a crimson-stained love letter to genre fiction" was exactly my intention, so I was glad to see that it came through for a reader.

Still, according to the definition we've just discussed, every work of fiction, indeed every work of literature, fits in one genre or another—so you might be wondering what Blom meant when he brought up "genre fiction" as if it were a specific type of fiction.

For a long time, *genre fiction* has been used as a derogatory term for stories that rely on the tropes of the fantastical, the sexual, or the violent. There was a belief that genre fiction was low art, of little socially redeeming value, and inferior to "literary fiction": for some, the mere fact that a novel could be labelled as, say, sci-fi or a romance meant that it could never truly be a "great" book.

But much of that condescension has fallen by the wayside. With Stephen King being awarded the Medal for Distinguished Contributions to American Letters, and J. K. Rowling selling nearly half a billion *Harry Potter* books and moving from poverty to being the twelfth richest woman in the United Kingdom, I think the term *genre fiction* no longer has the connotations that it once had.

The distinction between genre fiction and literary fiction is ignored by many, who may even be unaware of the terms or of their use to describe two possibly distinct classes of literature. In addition, the term *genre fiction* has been adopted by some writers and readers who do not share the belief that stories under that heading are unworthy art. The Internet, in particular, has done a really good job of flattening out what used to be the peaks and valleys separating "low art" and "high art"; today, we all have our own little niche tribes, and for the most part we are not ashamed to be part of them.

How Many Genres?

If you look up "List of literary genres" at Wikipedia, you'll find that there are dozens, divided into well over a hundred sub-genres. But that's far too many for our purposes and, especially in the case of genre fiction, virtually all of the genres can be rolled up into these big nine:

- *Crime* stories focus on criminal enterprise, told from the viewpoint of the perpetrators or of the crime-fighters working against them.

- **Fantasy** stories usually have magic or other supernatural element as the main ingredient in setting, plot, or theme.
- **Horror** stories try to frighten readers or disgust them. Often, but not always, the frightening element is supernatural, such as a demon, a monster, or witchcraft.
- **Inspirational** stories usually have religious belief as a major plot element or theme.
- **Melodramatic** stories generally have strongly emotional content, family trouble, conflict in school or the workplace, natural and man-made disasters, and adventures in nature (such as mountain-climbing).
- **Mystery/detective** stories usually are centred on the investigation of crime, often a murder or murders.
- **Romance** usually centres on two persons' mutual attraction and romantic love, with a happy ending.
- **Science fiction** stories tend to be at least semi-plausible depictions of the future, in which advances in scientific knowledge and technological engineering are important elements of setting, plot, or theme.
- **Western** stories usually are set in the American

West, often in the latter half of the 19th century, with cowboys as the heroes.

A Contract with Your Readers

Why should you focus on one of the big nine? When it comes to the novel, genre serves a very important function. It is a contract between the author and the reader: it establishes expectations that the book will provide the security of **generic conventions**[2] and the pleasure of the familiar, while limiting the risk of the unexpected. If you don't live up to your end of the contract by meeting your reader's expectations, the results can be unpredictable.

Genre provides stories with specific, codified elements of **iconography** and **narrative conventions**.

Iconography

Often, many typical icons are associated with a given genre. These can fall into several categories:

- **Character types** are one example; certain types of characters appear in certain types of stories.
- **Costume** can also play a huge role in a story, and is

---

[2]   These are the conventions that are part of the genre.

often dictated by genre. Think of the gowns that women wear to balls in Victorian melodramas, or the spacesuits worn in sci-fi stories.

- **Setting**, in both place and time, is determined largely by genre.
- **Tone** also is affected by genre; you probably are not going to write a grim and gritty "chick-lit" book, because such a tone works against the expectations and conventions of that genre.

If you depart from generic conventions in any of these areas, it can have strange effects on the reader.

When Ang Lee's film *Brokeback Mountain* was released, it was discussed everywhere in the media and over water coolers. Everyone I knew was talking about "the gay-cowboy movie". So, when I went to see the film, I was expecting a story set in the late 19th century and featuring gay cowboys in the Wild West! I had to spend the first ten or fifteen minutes of the film rearranging my expectations when I realized that that was *not* the case. The movie did not live up to my expectations of the generic conventions of chronologic setting, and that departure really hindered my initial enjoyment of the story, though I was eventually able to get myself situated in the modern setting of the narrative.

An opposite case took place with *Silver Linings Playbook*. Before I saw it, my understanding was that the film was a romantic comedy and therefore not something I would be especially interested in. When I finally viewed the movie, however, I was blown away to discover that it wasn't a romantic comedy at all—certainly not a traditional one, anyway. I was profoundly moved by the story (just try not to get weepy during the scene in which the main characters dance to Bob Dylan's "Girl from the North Country"), and I immediately purchased and read Matthew Quick's novel, from which the film was adapted. In the case of *Silver Linings Playbook*, a failure to live up to generic expectations brought me a peculiar form of surprised enjoyment, given that the conventions of the genre generally do not appeal to me. On the other hand, it is quite possible that a great number of readers and filmgoers who are fans of light romantic comedies were disappointed by the story's refusal to live up to generic expectations. My reaction, and those of other readers and viewers, demonstrate why the writer must handle genre with skill, knowledge, and intention.

Narrative Conventions

Genre isn't just about iconography. It's also about narrative conventions, which include a range of story traits:

- *Length* is a common consideration. An epic fantasy novel probably will be much longer than your fast-paced, breakneck thriller.
- *Plot devices* are often specific to genre, such as the magical helper character who saves the day at the

last minute in fantasy and science fiction.

- *Character actions*, such as a female protagonist's having to choose between a bad boy and a good boy in a chick-lit story, are common.
- *Story events*, such as an encounter with an extra-terrestrial species in a science-fiction novel, are often associated with particular genres.

Using Genre to Set Boundaries

All of these codified generic conventions play important roles both for your readers and for you. Genre provides your readers with a promise that you will meet their expectations. For you, the writer, genre limits the storytelling options.

As a writer, why would you want to *impose limitations* on yourself? Here is what Orson Welles, an extremely successful artist in several media, had to say on the topic:

" *The enemy of art is the absence of limitations.* "

When you're struggling with "writer's block", what is overcoming you isn't an *absence* of ideas. Thinking about *nothing* is really difficult: I'm sure you've had that experience of lying in bed, unable to sleep, even though you need to get up early and go to work the next day—you can't sleep because so many ideas just keep flowing through your mind. When you're dealing with writer's block, it's often similar: you don't *lack* ideas; rather, you're faced with *too many*. There are just too many possible ways to tell a story, and there is too vast a field of subjects and character types to choose from.

By consciously setting your novel in a specific genre, you're limiting your options and thereby making your story development easier.

Genre as Your Starting-Point

Author Larry Brooks has penned two excellent books on writing, *Story Engineering* and *Story Physics*, both of which I strongly encourage you to read. Brooks writes about the distinctions among three different things, which he terms *ideas*, *concepts*, and *premises*.

To get at what we mean by these three different terms, think of the following. "I want to write a book about a road trip." That's a great *idea*, but that's all it is—an idea. You need to develop it further. You need characters. "I want to write a story about a father and a son on a road trip." Okay, we're getting better: you now have a *concept*. But a concept is still missing the core conflict that drives a story. A much better place to start would be with the following *premise*: "My story is about a man with a terminal illness, travelling across Canada with his son, trying to make it from Halifax to Victoria before he dies." Boom! Now that's a half-decent starting point.

Yet, as Brooks points out in *Story Engineering*, whether your premise really is a good starting point depends largely on genre. What might be a great "high concept" idea in one genre could be run-of-the-mill in another.

A film about a superhero with an ex-girlfriend who is also a superhero herself isn't much of a concept. Many superheroes have girlfriends with superpowers, so there isn't all that much interesting about that concept. But what if we moved those characters to a traditional romantic comedy, where the protagonist was an everyday guy—but with a superhero ex-girlfriend? Suddenly you have something so high-concept that they base a Hollywood film on it: *My Super Ex-Girlfriend*!

Too many people think of idea, concept, and premise as where they should start their novel. But beginning your work in *genre* allows your premise to grow and evolve in a more organic and organized fashion.

You need to plant the seeds of your story in the soil of genre. It is the nurturing foundation that will allow the seeds to grow into a novel. Genre is what gives life and context to ideas, concepts, and premises, which is why it is the first step in our blueprint.

Genre Life Stages

Genres themselves, however, are not static things. They are constantly moving along a path, from a primitive state, to classical and then revisionist forms, and finally becoming so well developed and so well known that they can be parodied.

Let's look at the horror genre as an example, and the vampire novel as a specific sub-genre.

In 1819, John William Polidori published his short story "The Vampyre". This is the vampire genre in its most primitive form. By 1897, Bram Stoker had written and released the quintessential vampire story, *Dracula*, thereby ushering in the genre's classical period. By the mid 1970s, Stephen King had re-envisioned Stoker's Dracula character and set him loose in small-town America in the novel *'Salem's Lot*, thus producing a revisionist take on the genre. For parody, we can then look to something like Christopher Moore's 1995 book, *Bloodsucking Fiends*, a rather comedic take on the vampire genre.

Such evolution is not unique to the vampire sub-genre, or to horror in general: every genre goes through these stages. So you'll want to know where, culturally, your genre is in the cycle, and where in the cycle you will be placing your story. There's nothing wrong with writing a classical story while everyone else is publishing parodies, but you need to be *aware* that you'll be writing *against* the current generic expectations.

Different and Combined Perspectives

There is probably someone reading this right now thinking, "Christopher Moore's book isn't parody—it's revisionist! And *'Salem's Lot* has all the hallmarks of a classic vampire tale." That person might be you!

And you'd be totally right, because there are no absolutes when it comes to genres. A genre isn't a concrete thing: you can't pick it up and touch it. A genre is just a conceptual framework for ideas, a tool to organize your thinking and help you in your writing. Think of genre as a bag that you can group ideas in, so that you can pull them out when you need them and as you see fit.

There are no rules to writing fiction. If you want to write a western novel and set it in Halifax, Nova Scotia, go for it! (That sounds pretty high-concept, actually.) But you're still going to be rooted in the conventions of the western genre, and you can't subvert generic conventions until you've first acknowledged them as a starting-point.

Too many an inexperienced writer dives in to telling

a story without first thinking about and acknowledging where that kind of story is situated culturally, and where it has come from. Remember what Donne wrote: "No man is an island". The cultural history that inescapably precedes and surrounds you cannot be ignored. There is, however, no need to enslave yourself to generic conventions; just be aware of them, and then use them as you find appropriate.

In fact, some critics argue that the genius of an effective genre piece is in the variation, recombination, and evolution of the existing generic codes. If you have seen the film *Shaun of the Dead*, then you have an idea of how recombining generic codes can work effectively. By mixing a zombie movie with a romantic comedy, the filmmakers produced a rom-zom-com that felt surprisingly fresh and enjoyable.

Another example is the acclaimed television series *Firefly*. People often think of that show as "western meets sci-fi", which is a pretty fair description of the film that the series inspired, *Serenity*. But the genius of the original TV show was that every episode featured a mash-up of science fiction and some other genre, not just a western: there was a "medical drama meets sci-fi" episode, there was a "Victorian melodrama meets sci-fi" episode, and so on. You certainly can combine genres and have great success.

But, before you go too far down that road, let's recap what we've discussed in this chapter.

Summary

Genre is a contract between the writer and the reader. It provides the reader with specific expectations that you, the writer, will need to meet if you're going to uphold your end of that contract. Genre also functions as a helpful tool for the writer, because it limits storytelling options. Why would you want to limit the possibilities of your story? Because the absence of limitations is the enemy of art. You don't want to have to pull your story ideas from every possible option: that approach is too overwhelming. Genre gives you a sandbox to play in, rather than an endless desert. The more you mix genres together, the wider your storytelling options become—and, before long, you're lost in the void again.

For your first novel, I recommend sticking to a single genre in order to limit the options of your story and thereby make developing your story that much easier.

Homework

Choose which of the big nine genres you're going to use for your novel: crime, fantasy, horror, inspirational, melodrama, mystery/detective, romance, science fiction, or western.

Remember that you *don't* need any sort of specific idea, concept, or premise for a story at this stage; just choose the type of story you would like to tell.

Once you have settled on a genre, research that genre heavily. What are the classic texts of that genre? Find them and read them. What are the iconographic conventions of that genre? What are the narrative conventions? Who are the fans of that genre? What is it about the genre that attracts them? How will you live up to their expectations or depart from those conventions?

Step Two: Story Structure

This book is called THE NOVEL WRITER'S BLUEPRINT, so let's continue with the architectural metaphor for a moment. When building a house, you don't just start nailing up drywall out of nowhere: first you establish a foundation, upon which the rest of the house will be built later. In the case of novel-writing, as we discussed in Step One, genre is the foundation.

Next, in the construction of a house, a skeleton of studs, beams, and joists is fastened together to form a framework that holds everything else together. The skeleton of a novel is its story structure—Step Two of THE NOVEL WRITER'S BLUEPRINT.

Before we go any further, I want to ask you a simple question: *What basic structural elements does every story have?* This isn't a trick question, and the answer is straightforward and obvious. Yet, when I ask this question to my students in live workshops, they often say "conflict" or "character", but rarely do they call out the answer I'm looking for.

What Every Story Must Have

Every good story must have *a beginning, a middle, and an end*. If you have those three elements, then you have a story. If you're missing any of them, then you probably don't have a story. These essential elements are so obvious that many a beginning writer doesn't realize how important it is to give them serious thought, and to do it early in the project.

One perhaps obvious reason why the beginning and the end are important is that they provide hallmarks by which a story can become recognized instantly in the cultural memory. The moment we begin enjoying a story, one of our major concerns is to learn, eventually, how it ends; and so great is this concern that story titles can become cultural shorthand for the way an event turns out—recounting a dream, we might say, "It was like the end of *The Wizard of Oz*," and be understood immediately. Beginnings, too, are important, partly because they offer one of the earliest opportunities to attract and hold readers' attention, and partly because of their contributions to the wider culture. Genesis, the first book of the Bible, opens in a way that is both startlingly straightforward and known almost universally in Judeo-Christian society: "In the beginning". Charles Dickens started his novel *A Tale of Two Cities* with the memorable statement that "It was the best of times, it was the worst of times". Even the beginnings of books that are not very well known can still provide popular phrases, such as the first words of Richard Nixon's memoir, in which he declares, "I was born in a house my father built." So you can help your novel succeed by grabbing your readers' attention with a captivating opening and by leaving them with a memorable ending.

But there also are other, deeper reasons why you should think carefully about your story's beginning and end, and the middle that joins them. These reasons are matters not of theme, or tone, or character, but of basic structure. Just as visitors to your home would appreciate, at least subconsciously, having a definite sense that they were on the street, in your front yard, on the porch, or thoroughly indoors, so too will your readers appreciate a firm sense of what part of your story they have reached. Giving them this sense helps make it easy for them to enjoy the ride you're giving them, just as surely as sticking to generic conventions, as discussed in Step One, helps them know what to expect.

Think of some of the stories you've written, or portions of a larger manuscript that you've already drafted. Did you always know *exactly* which part of your story you were in while you were writing it? Did you know what signalled the transition from the beginning of your story to the middle, and from the middle to the end?

I hope you answered "Yes", but too often the answer is "No".

I'm reminded of studying D. W. Griffith in film school.

Griffith, one of the earliest master film directors, is credited with inventing the close-up. I remember reading that and thinking, "What? Someone had to *invent* the close-up?" It seems shocking, but it is absolutely true. Even the most obvious storytelling techniques have to be identified by *someone*—even the concept of a beginning, a middle, and an end. That three-part story structure was identified by Aristotle more than 2,300 years ago. The idea seems to have stuck around fairly well, so let's go with it.

Getting from A to Z

It's essential that you understand those three basic story parts when you're devising the plot of your narrative, because each part serves a unique purpose and requires unique story elements.

But, while agreement is pretty much universal that a story must start and finish, and that a middle must connect the beginning and the end, there is a much greater variety of thinking on how far inward the beginning and end each should stretch, and what the journey between them should look like—how many waypoints there are, and the nature of the legs that connect them.

Taking a Cue from Hollywood

One of the simplest ways of discussing the concept of a beginning, a middle, and an end for a story is to talk of Act I, Act II, and Act III.

If you've looked even a little into screenwriting techniques, you probably immediately recognize those three acts as the **Hollywood Three-Act Structure.** This is the classic script structure that aspiring screenwriters are told to follow when trying to write the next summer blockbuster. There are endless resources on this topic, with Syd Field and Robert McKee being two of the best-regarded writers and instructors on screenwriting.

The idea of story structure is absolutely essential in the world of screenwriting, and it happens to be where I got my start in long-form creative writing. I think those early years of immersion in the world of cinema and screenwriting might explain my affinity for an organized approach to novel-writing. In writing movies, there are no wasted pages. By page ten you need your major conflict established, and by page eighty you sure as heck better be headed into your third act.

Of course, there are certain screenwriters, such as Quentin Tarantino, Aaron Sorkin, and David Mamet, who are more interested in the poetry of language than in the typical three acts. But the average blockbuster depends heavily on a rigidly structured story.

The length of a screenplay is limited by external forces

that novels are not bound by. Originally, the length of a motion picture was determined by the length of film that could fit in a camera or projector. Later, when multi-reel films were being shot and exhibited, other factors came into consideration, such as the commercial interests of the theatres projecting the films: the two-hour length of the average movie was settled on largely because of the number of screenings a theatre could get in during a single day and how high a price moviegoers were willing to pay for a ticket; films longer than two hours cut too far into ticket sales.

Because of the external factors that restrict screenwriting, the importance of structure is heavily emphasized in that field. But, in writing that will be consumed ultimately as written words, we don't hear enough about structure—and that's a shame, because, as a novelist, you should embrace story structure. You may even want to push that idea a little further than merely dividing your tale into three acts.

The *bridge structure* is a simple way of doing this. Imagine the three spans of a suspension bridge. You still have a story broken into three acts (the beginning, the middle, and the end); but you now also have the two tower-topped piers serving as the major *plot points* (the thresholds your characters must cross), thereby signalling the changes between the acts.

Plot Point 1, marking the transition from Act I to Act II, is one of the most important moments in your novel, because it is the moment when your protagonist's life changes

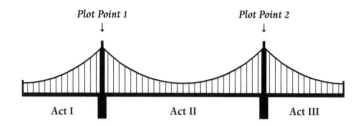

Figure 2. Suspension bridge representing Hollywood Three-Act Structure, with two plot points.

forever. It's the moment when your novel kicks in to high gear, and your character begins responding to the new state of the world and the various challenges therein. The rest of Act II will be spent in an effort to achieve one or more goals, whether it's the protagonist's effort to overcome her inner demons, the knight's attempt to rescue the princess, or a community's pulling together in the face of a natural disaster.

Plot Point 2 usually is your climax. All exposition has been communicated by this point in the story, and the tension and stakes have reached their peak. This is the moment when the villain is defeated, the mission is accomplished, and the world is saved. Your main character crosses another threshold, returning to the world in which he or she began, but having been changed by these experiences.

In a suspension bridge, the middle span is longer than each of the other two. Similarly, a common feature of the

Hollywood Three-Act Structure is that Act II is the longest, while Acts I and III pass by relatively quickly. The same formula can work in your novel, quickly hooking readers with a conflict that arises early in the story, and not dragging things on too long once the climax has passed.

James Scott Bell has a *Writer's Digest* tutorial in which he discusses this bridge structure in depth, and one of the fascinating ideas he covers is that Act II, the middle portion of the bridge, is the **valley of death**. He argues that, during the middle portion of the story, your protagonist must be confronted by death. Sometimes it is physical death; but it can also be emotional, spiritual, psychological, or professional death.

Four Acts under the Big Top

Larry Brooks, mentioned earlier, argues for a **tent structure**, which essentially stretches the bridge into four acts by adding a plot point in the middle of what would be Act II in the bridge structure. This new point marks a shift in the character's response, from passivity to action.

For Brooks, the four parts of the story are (1) the **set-up**, which establishes the world, characters, and stakes of your novel; (2) the **response**, which is your main character's initial reaction to a change that the world has undergone; (3) the **attack**, which follows the **mid-point** and signals your character's first effort against these new challenges; and (4) the **resolution** of the narrative, which follows the climax at the end of the third part.

Brooks also includes two mid-act *pinch points*—one each in Part 2 and Part 3—which I like to think of as simply the moments when the villain gets some screen time. Pinch Point 1 might be the first time you cut away from your protagonist and reveal the antagonistic forces at play in your novel. Pinch Point 2 is often your character's lowest moment, where defeat seems certain, just before the hero finds the ability to carry on to victory despite the odds.

Another way to approach Brooks's four-part structure is from a character perspective, in which the four parts can be described as *orphan*, *wanderer*, *warrior*, and *martyr*.

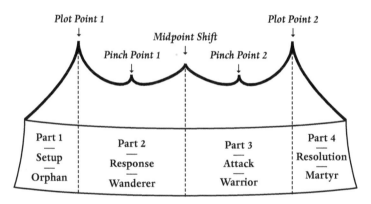

Figure 3. Larry Brooks's Tent Structure.

In describing Part 4 as the martyr portion of the story, Brooks isn't suggesting that your character *must* die; but your protagonist does need to be *willing* to die, willing to give up everything for the greater good. (Remember, we aren't necessarily talking about physical death.)

Five Acts and a Pyramid

If you want to push beyond the four-act structure, you can use five acts. There was a writer a few years back who had a great deal of success building each of his stories in five acts, and his work is still extremely popular. His name? William Shakespeare.

But it's not as if Shakespeare invented the five-act story—it was the established story structure in much of Renaissance theatre. In terms of structure and form, he wasn't pushing the boundaries of his medium. Nor were his plots especially original: most were adapted from stories that had already been popular for a number of years and from historical tales. What separated Shakespeare from other writers was the unique vision and mastery of language that he brought to those already established characters, events, and structures.

In the middle of the 19th century, Gustav Freytag, a German academic, analyzed Ancient Greek drama and the work of Shakespeare and other playwrights, and concluded that most such plays had five parts: (1) the **introduction**; (2) the *rise*; (3) the *climax*; (4) the **return**, or the *fall*; and (5) the *catastrophe* (conclusion). At the juncture between the introduction and the rise lay the first *crisis* (turning-point), which he described as an *exciting moment* or *exciting force*; the second crisis, the *tragic moment* or *tragic force*, marked the end of the climax and the beginning of the fall; and the third crisis, the *moment* (or *force*) *of last suspense*, marked the transition from the fall to the catastrophe. Freytag loosely tied these five parts of story action to the five acts of Shakespeare's plays, and showed how the same five-part sequence played out in one- and three-act works.

Since then, others have offered their own versions of *Freytag's Pyramid*. One result is that the pyramid and Shakespeare's five acts are sometimes taken to be one and the same, the five parts firmly tied in one-to-one correspondence with the five acts. Other changes to Freytag's Pyramid include the depiction of the climax as a *point*, rather than a part of some *length*; changes in vocabulary; and the introduction of additional pieces in the pyramid. The illustration on page 54 attempts to reconcile these variations; but this cannot be done perfectly, because there are contradictions among the different models.

Sometimes, this general view, of a tragedy as progressing from a low point, passing through a peak, and returning to a low, is called the *dramatic arc*.

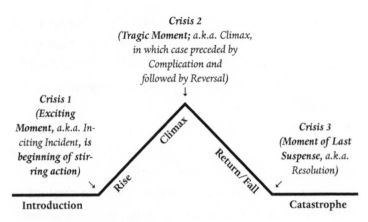

Figure 4. Freytag's Pyramid, with modifications.

A Shared Essence

You've probably noticed similarities among all the structures discussed so far. Indeed, we might even say that they completely overlap one another. This is because they're all

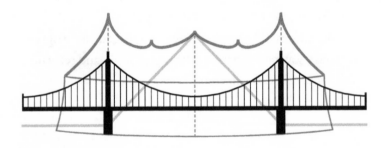

Figure 5. Hollywood Three-Act Structure, Larry Brooks's Tent, and Freytag's Pyramid, overlapping one another.

ways of identifying, organizing, and articulating the essential, *common* elements of story structure.

The Monomyth, or the Hero's Journey

You may already be familiar with Joseph Campbell's story-structure concept—the monomyth, or hero's journey. He arrived at this concept after studying many of the world's long-lived myths, and described the result in his famous book *The Hero with a Thousand Faces*. This structure is often mentioned in connection with George Lucas, who credits much of the success of the first *Star Wars* film he made to its adherence to Campbell's story structure, in which the "hero ventures forth from the world of common day into a region of supernatural wonder: fabulous forces are there encountered and a decisive victory is won: the hero comes back from this mysterious adventure with the power to bestow boons on his fellow man".

The hero's journey usually is depicted in a circular format, as opposed to the linear diagrams of Hollywood, Brooks, and Freytag. But, if you look closely, you'll find that it's just another take on Aristotle's three-act structure: Campbell identifies a *departure*, an *initiation*, and a *return*. Each of these large acts has various steps within itself: Campbell identified seventeen possible steps, but also found that very few myths used all seventeen steps; and, since then, other analysts have reworked his concept, variously adding, subtracting, and combining steps, and renam-

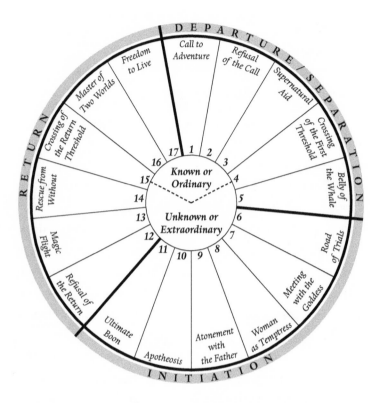

Figure 6. Joseph Campbell's Monomyth, or Hero's Journey.

ing them. These variations may be good food for thought when you're deciding just what phases your protagonist will go through on the path from your story's beginning to its end, so look them up. You have many named parts available to use, in case you want them.

Propp's Steps

In fact, twenty years before Campbell did his work, a Russian folklorist, Vladimir Propp, published *Morphology of the Folktale*. After analyzing the canon of Russian folk stories, Propp identified a story structure of thirty-one steps (!) that he argued served as the framework for most Russian folktales.

This is exactly why I suggest you'll never have to face writer's block again! Next time you don't know what story to tell, head over to Wikipedia and look up *Morphology of the Folktale* or, better yet, read the book. Propp's thirty-one steps are just waiting for you to put them to use. All you need to do is bring your unique perspective to that structure.

Harmon's Circle

If you don't want to go all the way back to 1920s Russia, you can turn your attention to someone a little more recent: Dan Harmon, creator of the television sitcom *Community*. Harmon came up with a story structure, also represented as a circle, through which he walked his character for one episode after another—and yet, I believe, virtually everyone would agree that *Community* is one of the *least* formulaic sitcoms. *Formula* does not have to mean *formulaic*!

For homework, go watch an episode of *Community*, preferably from one of the earlier seasons, and try to identify each of these stages of the story: a character (1) is in a zone

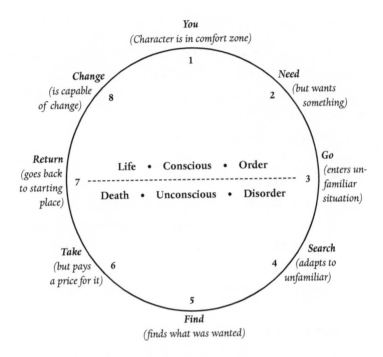

Figure 7. Dan Harmon's circular story structure.

of comfort, but (2) wants something and (3) enters an unfamiliar situation, (4) adapts to it, and (5) finds what he or she wanted, but (6) has to pay a price, and (7) finally returns to the place from which he or she started, now (8) either changed or at least capable of change.

The Effectiveness of Structure

I am not saying that your tale *must* be tied to any particular one of these story frameworks; but your narrative must have internal coherence, and that's what the story structures we have discussed here provide. It worked for Shakespeare, it worked for George Lucas, and it can work for you, too.

Even if you aspire to write radically experimental novels, you'll still need to keep these concepts in mind. José Saramago's novel *Blindness*, for example, is rather avant-garde: none of the characters in the book has a name; quotation marks aren't used for dialogue; there are huge, chapter-long paragraphs; commas replace periods throughout the book. And yet, if you look closely, you find that *Blindness* is structured by three distinct acts: there is a beginning, where an epidemic of blindness spreads rapidly; this is followed by a middle, in which the characters are locked together in an asylum; and finally there is an end, in which the protagonists re-enter the world as new people, changed by their experiences in the asylum—where, of course, they faced death.

For another example of the effectiveness of structure, let's return to John Donne's *Meditations*. I've already mentioned the "No man is an island" quote several times, but what you may not know is that the familiar phrase "for whom the bell tolls" also is from that same passage of *Meditations*. Clearly, this is an extremely memorable and moving part of Donne's work.

Structurally, *Meditations* consists of twenty-three chronologically ordered sections, representing the length, in days, of the severe illness that Donne had survived. Each section contains (1) a "meditation", in which he describes a stage of his sickness; (2) an "expostulation", containing his reaction to that stage; and (3) a "prayer", in which he makes peace with the disease.

Donne's *Meditations* is rooted in genre (specifically, inspirational writing), and follows a highly structured format; yet, the work he produced was not formulaic. Nor was it forgettable: rather, by using genre and structure, Donne produced a piece of literature that we're still talking about four hundred years later—and it has not one, but two, lines that are often quoted in everyday 21st-century speech.

We should all strive to write something one tenth as profound.

Homework

In addition to doing the *Community* assignment on pages 57–58, identify which of the story structures discussed here appeals to you. We have only brushed the surface of these structures—so, once you've chosen the one you'll use for your novel, read up and make sure you learn all the intricacies of your chosen structure.

Step Three: Puzzle Work

Puzzle work probably isn't a term you're too familiar with, especially in the craft of novel-writing: it's the name I give to an approach I've developed myself. I haven't seen anything quite like it described elsewhere, and yet it has proven extremely helpful in the writing of my novels.

Puzzle work is almost the complete opposite of the traditional approach. Rather than begin developing your novel with a premise or a character, I recommend you start laying out your plot by identifying the key *moments* that you want to have in your story. These moments might be based on ones from the stories you love.

Think of it as building a jigsaw puzzle. First you can pick out some key parts—the corners, the edges, and maybe a large and easy-to-build part of the picture that connects to an edge. Once you have those key sections identified and placed, you begin filling in all the little details that join those larger sections together into one coherent whole.

The Big Puzzle Pieces

I once read a review of Quentin Tarantino's film *Pulp Fiction* in which the reviewer said something like "This director just takes the best scenes from other movies, and gets rid of everything else, so it's nothing but back-to-back great scenes." The reviewer wrote as if Tarantino were cheating by filling his movies with all the good stuff from other stories! Such criticism is ironic, given that film critics tend to love Alfred Hitchcock, who is often quoted as saying that movies are real life with all the boring bits edited out.

But that's film, and we can't quite replicate that approach when writing a book. Long-form novels, in particular, need to ebb and flow; they need calmer, quieter moments mixed with high-intensity moments. Constant intensity can be found in the work of some writers, such as Chuck Palahniuk; but he is a master minimalist, and therefore able to get away with it in a way that probably is beyond the ability of the average novelist. For the most part, if your novel has a handful of high-impact scenes, you're doing just fine.

Puzzle work is about putting into practice the modelling we discussed in the INTRODUCTION. For your homework there, you identified some of your favourite moments and scenes from books, films, television, and/or theatrical productions, especially scenes you would like to mimic or pay homage to in your novel. Now you're going to use those favourite moments as models for your big puzzle pieces, the big scenes that you will try to emulate in your book. If your story is going to have a particular scene, obviously it must *lead* to that scene. Thus, choosing scenes is similar to selecting the places that you will visit during a road trip: once you've chosen the sights to see, you are forced to devise ways of getting to them.

One of my favourite scenes in literature is the moment in *The Great Gatsby* when the title character stands outside of Daisy's house, concerned for her safety and waiting for her to come out into the night. She is never going to come out, and he is never going to be able to enter truly into the upper-class world whose acceptance he desires so desperately. He'll always be excluded; and he'll never have Daisy, his one true love. More recently, I was very moved by the moment in *The Hunger Games* when Katniss is sent a loaf of bread by District 11, in reciprocation for the kindness she has shown to their competitor, Rue. These are the types of memorable, enchanting moments I try to work in to my novels.

Identify the moments that have moved you. These will become the big puzzle pieces around which you will build your narrative. The big pieces don't necessarily have to be individual scenes; they can also be sequences of scenes, stylistic flourishes, single lines of dialogue—even simply feelings.

There is an episode of *Buffy the Vampire Slayer* in which the protagonist is videotaped by another character while going about her vampire-slaying. The cameraman explains Buffy's mission as "a story of ultimate triumph tainted with the bitterness for what's been lost in the struggle." That line struck me deeply, because it perfectly articulated the *feeling* I almost always aim at in the conclusions of my stories. I hope that, when readers finish *The Page Turners*, they have experienced "ultimate triumph tainted with the bitterness for what's been lost in the struggle." I think I first experienced this feeling myself, as a reader, at the conclusion of Tolkien's *The Return of the King*, where it becomes clear that the wounds that Frodo has suffered along his journey will never heal: it is a triumph for the Hobbits, but a tainted one.

To see what I mean by **stylistic flourish**, check out the middle portion of a great Virginia Woolf novel, *To the Lighthouse*. This part of the book is called "Time Passes"; it covers a span of ten years, largely by describing the interior of an empty house. It's a memorable, absolutely beautiful passage, something I would love to emulate.

Rather than stare into the void, hoping the muse arrives to give you a perfect premise on which to base your entire novel, build your story by taking those big, passionate, shocking, exciting, and memorable moments, and then—hang them on the skeleton of your chosen story structure.

To a certain extent, logic and a bit of strategic thinking will dictate where in the structure those scenes will need to be placed. If the moment you want to model is a big battle in which the villain is vanquished, it probably belongs near the climax of your chosen structure. If one of your favourite moments is a scene in which a main character is introduced, it probably belongs somewhere in Act I.

Filling In the Gaps

Once the big scenes have been placed in your structure, it's time for the real puzzle work to begin. That means you can now (finally!) put on your artist's hat.

Filling in the gaps can be completed using a ***beat-sheet***, a simple list of your story's scenes in chronological order from beginning to end. Generally, one starts with a bullet list of descriptions and builds from there; but you should feel free to include as little or as much detail as you want. You'll probably have more details for your big-puzzle-piece scenes from the get-go than you will for your gap-filling scenes. It's in developing the beat-sheet and filling in the gaps between the big pieces that you'll need to be creative and strategic to ensure that everything fits together. *How* will your characters *get* from point A to point B, so that you have an actual story in which to place those moments you love from your favourite works?

In addition to moving characters around the chessboard that is your story structure, you may also want to associate specific objects with certain characters early in your story, and then move those objects to other characters. What happens when an object has moved from one character to another? When Bilbo ends up with Gollum's ring, what is the result? What happens when Daisy gets behind the wheel of Gatsby's car, or when the magic slippers end up on Dorothy's feet? The transfer of an object can radically change a story's trajectory.

Much of the time, doing your puzzle work will involve coming up with answers to the question "Why don't they just _____?" Why don't they just *not* go into the haunted house? Why don't they just call for help? Why doesn't she just find another guy? Why doesn't he just quit his job? Why doesn't she move to the far side of the universe, where the villain won't bother her? Why don't they just let the secret be known?

On this topic, author Rainbow Rowell has a pretty funny quote, concerning cell phones:

> " *There's nothing worse for plots than cellphones. Once your characters have one, there's no reason for them to get lost or stranded. Or miss each other at the top of the Empire State Building. If you want anything like that to happen, you either have to explain upfront what happened*

> *to the phones or you have to make at least one
> character some sort of manic pixie Luddite who
> doesn't carry one.* "

That's not only funny, but also quite accurate. Why *doesn't* your character have a cell phone? Having to answer such questions can be limiting; but, as you already know from Step One, limiting your storytelling options can actually be extremely helpful.

My novel *The Page Turners* is about teenagers who are battling a vicious, powerful killer. While plotting it, I was constantly forced to grapple with the question *Why don't the teens just go to the police for help?* Ultimately, I decided there was no avoiding it: the kids would *have* to go to the police. But, in order for the story to work, their plea for help would have to be ignored.

That requirement, in turn, led me to the question of why the police would refuse to help. Well, maybe the policeman they were dealing with wasn't a good person, I thought. Maybe he was actually a full-on villain, somehow connected to the larger plot. The character of Sergeant Alderwood, and an entire subplot involving him, thus evolved from the need to answer "Why don't they just _____?" questions.

Another question that writers are often forced to confront during the puzzle work is why the hero doesn't just run away from all the challenges. You'll find that, more often than not, there is an extremely strong connection established between the protagonist and the antagonist in a story. Luke Skywalker *must* face Darth Vader, *because Vader is his father*. Harry Potter *cannot* just run away from Voldemort, *because they are psychically connected*, existing within each other's minds no matter how great the physical distance between them. Consider making a similar connection between your antagonist and protagonist. At the very least, determine why your hero doesn't simply run away.

We've already emphasized the need for story structure in the arc of your whole narrative. But, during your puzzle work, you'll need to remember that each *scene* also must have structure, though you'll have a little more leeway in terms of shortening or extending sections.

If you want a scene to be exciting, for example, you may want to skip most of its beginning (Act I of the scene) and get right to the conflict of the middle (Act II of the scene). However, if you want to draw out the tension (if, for example, there's a bomb under the table that the reader knows about but the hero is unaware of), you may want to give the scene a long introduction.

In addition, try to ensure that every scene in your book either reveals character, or moves the plot forward by providing one piece of exposition. If the scene is not doing one of those two things, both your scene and your overall narrative might have a problem.

Summary

Now it's time to review what we've covered so far in THE NOVEL WRITER'S BLUEPRINT.

You've picked a genre, which is the foundation upon which you're going to build your narrative; the genre limits your storytelling possibilities and has given you a well defined sandbox to play in. You then chose which of the established story structures to use to organize your narrative. You've identified the big puzzle pieces in your story, the moments you're highly drawn to including. You've placed those big scenes against your chosen structure, and now you've begun filling in the gaps between the big pieces, always keeping in mind the iconographic and narrative conventions of your chosen genre.

What I hope you've noticed is that, through this process, your premise and characters have begun to evolve naturally and organically, because of story requirements. Your story-building is expanding in all directions, developing as it goes. Using this system, you aren't starting with a single idea and pressing forever against that wall of the unknown, inching ever so slowly towards that single goal of reaching the ending. Instead, you're placing moments against a structure that is already proven to work with readers, and filling in the moments in between, thereby plotting your story in a far more organized and strategic manner.

Homework

Complete both parts of the puzzle work: place the big puzzle pieces on your structure, and fill in the gaps. When this process is complete, your story should have emerged, and a structured beat-sheet listing most of your book's major scenes should have been developed. If you are struggling, revisit the detailed story requirements of your chosen structure.

Step Four: Preparatory Regimen

In Steps One, Two, and Three of THE NOVEL WRITER'S BLUEPRINT, you focused on story-planning. With those steps completed, it's time to move into a transitional phase, with Step Four, the PREPARATORY REGIMEN. This is where we leave behind the plotting, the mere listing of the story sequence, and begin the creative writing.

A couple years ago, I managed to lose about forty pounds over several months. This fat loss was a transformative experience for me, and not just literally: I realized that I was in control of my body, and that all I needed to do to lose weight, get fit, and feel better was to educate myself and then take the necessary action. The lessons of sport and fat loss are the same lessons you can apply to the production of your novel, so we're going to use a bit of a sports metaphor for the this chapter and the next.

Before you read any further, I want you to take a moment and acknowledge that *you are in control of your life and your body*. It is such things as self-control, knowledge, support, practice, and organization that will allow you to be successful both in fitness and in novel-writing.

If you've skipped ahead at all, you know that Step Five is RUNNING THE MARATHON. Well, no one just jumps in to running a marathon: most people train for at least six months before tackling their first race. Yet, for some reason, people think they can just dive in to writing a novel without any preparation. You wouldn't expect to finish a marathon, let alone win it, without proper preparation—so you'll want to keep in mind the saying uttered in locker rooms and training facilities almost every day:

> " *The more you sweat in practice,*
> *the less you bleed in battle.* "

Regardless of their specific sport, all athletes have a regimen that prepares them for competition. This regimen consists of three elements: (1) diet, (2) training, and (3) rest and recovery. You need to have all three of these elements properly aligned during preparation if you're going to be a champion in sport—and the same is true in writing.

Element 1: Diet

Diet is what you take in to your body. You need proper nutrition in order to lose weight and get fit. I succeeded in my fat loss by following the Slow-Carb Diet, outlined in Timothy Ferriss's book *The 4-Hour Body*. As discussed in our introduction, Ferriss's book *The 4-Hour Chef* played a big role in the development of THE NOVEL WRITER'S BLUEPRINT; but *The 4-Hour Body* had an even greater influence on my life, by introducing me to diet and exercise.

The Slow-Carb Diet involves eating only meat and vegetables six days a week, and then having a weekly epic cheat day, when you eat absolutely anything you want. This was the regimen for my fat loss, and now it's going to be the regimen for your literary diet as you prepare to write your novel.

The vegetables of your literary diet are workshops, online courses, conversations with mentors, and educational books—like the one you're reading now. Not everyone is interested in studying the mechanics of writing, and not everyone loves eating vegetables either; but you need them in order to be healthy.

Certainly, some things can be learned just by doing them. You can jump right in to the writing of your novel and learn as you go. That's what I did—but it took years, and I don't want you to have to learn these lessons the way I learned them. So your vegetables will be the education portion of your regimen.

The meat of your diet is great literature. To be a great writer, you need to be a great reader. That means reading the classic novels. Of course, everyone has his or her own definition of "the classics"; but you can hardly go wrong with the likes of Charlotte Brontë, F. Scott Fitzgerald, Thomas Hardy, Joseph Heller, Ernest Hemingway, and Virginia Woolf. These names have stood the test of time. You can look up any list of the top one hundred books of all time, and there's a good chance you'll find most of those names there.

I also encourage you to read the classics of your specific genre, along with its recent bestsellers. If you're writing a chick-lit novel, for example, you probably should have read *Bridget Jones's Diary*. If you're putting together a fantasy, you'd better have the *Narnia* books and *The Lord of the Rings* on your bookshelf. When I was in the final stages of writing *The Page Turners*, I went back and re-read *'Salem's Lot*.

One of the reasons why the Slow-Carb Diet works so well is the allowance for **one cheat day a week**. If you're having cravings (as we all do when dieting), the longest you ever have to wait to fulfill that craving is six days. It's not as if you have to stop eating pizza for the rest of your life: you just have to limit it to one day a week.

You'll do the same thing with your literary diet. Yes, you'll focus primarily on the general classics and on your chosen genre's classics and modern bestsellers; but you can also include one cheat day a week, to experience reading and other entertainment purely for pleasure. This can include magazines, blog articles, television, and movies.

I'm not suggesting that television and movies are worthless junk food in terms of stories (I'm a huge fan of both those media), but they are *undeniably* time-vacuums. We're going to talk a lot about optimizing time later on in the book; but, for now, just be aware that you need to limit that sort of stuff and that you can think of it, to an extent, as junk food. It's probably not going to help you much in your novel-writing; but, like a great pizza once a week, it might keep you sane!

Element 2: Training

If diet is what you put in to your body, training is your output. In the novel-writing world, you can think of training simply as *writing practice.* Through regular use of writing exercises you can develop your skills both before and during the drafting of your novel.

Mind-Mapping and Brainstorming

Most people have done some form of mind-mapping or brainstorming at some point, while developing an idea for a story or other project. There are apps, websites, and other software that can help you with this process, but you don't need modern technology. **Brainstorming** is just a way of jotting down ideas and making connections to get your writing started, before you have to worry about the specifics of overarching narrative, chapters, scenes, or even proper sentences. It helps limber up your mind and develop ideas you might otherwise have filtered out. Brainstorming is less organized than *mind-mapping*, in which one idea branches off into related ideas.

Timed Writing

Another approach to practice writing is timed writing exercises. You can set a timer for a specific period, such as five, ten, or fifteen minutes, and then you just keep that pen moving across the page, or fingers typing away at the keyboard, for the duration. You cannot stop. You must simply keep writing whatever flows out of you until the timer goes off. You'll be amazed by what will come out of you and by how many of those half-formed and fragmented ideas can be put together and used in your novel.

Writing down the Page

This is an exercise I am a huge fan of; I use it for the first draft of almost every one of my scenes. Normally, you write *across* the page; but, when writing *down* the page, you're not crafting full paragraphs, or even full sentences. Instead, you're just trying to capture the general flow of how the chapter you plan to write is going to play out. It's like developing a beat-sheet for a scene, rather than for your whole novel. Here's an example:

" *Our hero walks into the room.*
It's dark.
She senses something is off.
Is someone in the corner?
"Who's there?"
No answer.
(Tone: Tense/moody. Give it a noir feel.)
"I said, 'Who's there?'"
Still no answer.
Slight movement in corner of her eye . . .
The killer is in the corner!   "

In a sense, writing down the page is a brainstorming exercise, but one that follows the chronology of the chapter. It's part brainstorming, part story-planning—and, most important of all, it allows you to fill up that blank screen *fast!* When you write down the page, before you know it, you're staring at a long list of moments, feelings, descriptions, and bits of dialogue. Rather than grappling with the existential angst of the blank page, your project is the fleshing out of ideas that are already on the page and the crafting of crisp sentences—a much less daunting task than filling the void with paragraph after paragraph of prose right from the start.

Backstory

Backstory allows you to flesh out your story, setting, and characters without having to worry about whether any of the information will actually be used. It's a creative writing exercise focused on information that might never make it in to the novel, but could lead to discoveries or revelations that you, as the writer, *will* use. Even if none of the information is ever provided to the reader, sometimes just having characters' backstory in your own mind can help you to script their dialogue and plot their actions. Writers on many a television show (a format of storytelling in which multiple authors contribute to a single, ongoing story) develop a **story bible**, a reference guide identifying backstory elements, details of characters and settings, and established rules of the story's universe, which writers can refer to in order to avoid continuity errors. Your backstory efforts can evolve into a similar sort of reference guide, or can unravel in the form of long-form narrative, stand-alone short stories, or simple lists of ideas related to the theme of your story or the lives of your characters. By practicing your writing within the context of your novel's world, you're simultaneously working on your skill development and your novel development at the same time. Whenever you can combine the two tasks, it's all the more effective a use of your time.

Prompts

Writing in response to prompts can be another great exercise, and the Internet is full of writing-prompt resources. You can visit websites that offer a different prompt every day, and you can sign up for email lists that send prompts to your inbox every morning. These prompts are just sentences (sometimes unfinished) that are meant to inspire a short piece of writing.

One day's prompt might be "You wake up in a strange bed with a dead body next to you. How did it get there, and what happens next?"

These prompts can spark story ideas that you might not otherwise have considered.

Prompts can also be used to "get the juices flowing". So can all of the exercises discussed under this, the TRAINING heading. Writing is no different from sport. Hockey players don't just step on the ice and immediately drop the puck. First they warm up, to stretch out the kinks and get their blood pumping. Warming up is also necessary for writing. I guarantee you that the best line you write on any given day will not be the first line you write.

Short Stories

Short stories are an art form in and of themselves, and Canadian writer Alice Munro recently won the Nobel Prize for her short stories alone. But short stories can also be used both as writing exercises and as inspiration for longer narratives. The famous young-adult novel *Ender's Game* began as a short story; and Raymond Chandler's first book, *The Big Sleep*, was the amalgamation of two previously published short stories into a single, novel-length narrative. Ernest Hemingway, one of the greatest writers of all time, wrote stand-alone short stories, some of which ended up being incorporated into chapters of his novels. And novels such as John Steinbeck's *The Pastures of Heaven* and Ray Bradbury's *The Martian Chronicles* consist of seemingly stand-alone short stories that, when bound together and read in order, eventually reveal themselves to be all part of one ongoing, interconnected narrative.

Reference Images

A great exercise that I discovered while writing *The Page Turners* is to use the vast library of images that Google makes available. You can use this both as a practice tool, and in the crafting of your novel when you get stuck. For example, at one point in my novel, I needed to describe the interior of a barn, and I was having trouble coming up with the authentic details to really sell the environment to the reader. So I went to Google Images and typed something like "interior of big wooden barn", and dozens of photos came up. From there, I just had to describe, in writing, what I saw in those images.

When my editor and colleague, Forrest Adam Sumner, drew the maps of Maplewright that appear on the opening pages of *The Page Turners*, he also used the Web, specifically Google Maps, to find aerial and satellite photos of buildings, farms, parks, and roads in several North American cities and towns; he then combined these elements in a new way, bringing that much more realism to an imaginary place. Illustrators and painters constantly draw from models and reference photos; as a writer, you should be ready to embrace the same technique.

Poetry

You may be surprised to read this, but poetry is a marvellous way to work on your writing. Often, verse reveals things that would never come out in prose. In the case of *The Page Turners*, while writing a scene late in the book, I found myself falling into stanzas of poetry describing the hideousness of Maplewright, the town in which the novel is set. I went on for line after line, and the ideas just kept coming. What I ended up with was a long poem; but I couldn't have my novel just break into poetry three quarters of the way through—so I took elements of that poem and sprinkled those ideas throughout the book. Those little descriptions added life, colour, and texture to the novel, thereby enriching the description of the town and giving it the feeling of a real place. Indeed, it was this sense of realism in the prose that inspired my editor to draw the detailed maps of Maplewright. All this added one more level of authenticity to the story's setting, and thus to everything that took place there—and it probably never would have happened without that exploration in poetry.

Element 3: Rest and Recovery

Diet and exercise are each of major importance to the preparatory regimen, but you cannot forget the third element—rest and recovery. What we're really talking about here is *health*.

Your health.

Ask any strength-training athlete and you'll hear that **periodization** is an essential component of training. These athletes need to plan their training carefully, so that it includes both low- and high-intensity periods. They need to be regular in their programming in order to make it a habit and get their reps in, but they can't go all out all the time. That approach inevitably leads to burnout. The human body needs time to recover.

When discussing his approach to writing, Hemingway said this:

> " *The best way is always to stop when you are going good and when you know what will happen next. If you do that every day when you are writing a novel you will never be stuck.* "

You need to know when to stop.

James Wedmore, famous for his YouTube videos on marketing, started his entrepreneurial ventures as a writer. He tells a story about locking himself in his apartment and writing all day long for three months straight. He got his first book from that process and it launched his career, but he lost a girlfriend along the way. Locking yourself in a room for three months isn't a great thing for romantic relationships.

I started this book by saying that the creation of a novel is a life-and-death battle—so let's not forget the *life* part. Rest, recovery, and simple fun with friends and loved ones are indispensable to your overall health. If you lock yourself away and focus solely on your book, as James Wedmore did, you're going to hurt your relationships with loved ones.

I don't want to get too didactic, and I know this isn't necessarily what you signed up for when you purchased a book about novel-writing; but I feel a responsibility to give you the following advice:

- Get regular exercise.
- Get enough sleep.
- Eat real food.
- Have sex.
- Give your loved ones the focus and energy that they deserve.

Never forget that, while your novel needs your attention, other things take priority over it. This is the stuff that *really* matters in life.

Yes, finishing that chapter is important—but probably not as important as a good night's sleep. If you don't have your health, then that chapter you stayed up all night writing to completion . . . well, it could be the last chapter you ever write.

Homework

Try each of the exercises described in this section: mind-mapping, brainstorming, timed writing, writing down the page, coming up with backstory, writing to prompts, composing short stories, using reference images, and writing verse. Identify which ones feel right to you, and start making them part of your regular writing practice.

Step Five: Running the Marathon

Nicely done! You've made it all the way to Step Five, RUNNING THE MARATHON.

This chapter is broken down into four key challenges faced by writers during the drafting process. We're also going to beat every one of those challenges. Here they are:

1. Writing a novel is hugely time-consuming.
2. Writing a novel can be an extremely lonely effort.
3. Writing a novel is such a massive project that it can be too intimidating to even start.
4. Once you've started drafting, it can be extremely difficult to stick with it to completion.

There are thousands of writers with nothing more than half-written novels out there—but that isn't going to be *you*, because you're going to develop systems that help you carry on to the end!

Challenge 1: Writing a Novel Is Hugely Time-Consuming

HOW TO BEAT IT: Good time management!

How long does it take to produce a final draft of your writing? My analysis of my own work suggests that, including initial drafting, revising, and polishing, it takes about five hours to finish just a thousand words. That means that even a short, 50,000-word novel requires about 250 hours of work!

How do you possibly find 250 hours to write in this crazy, fast-paced world of ours?

I'm sure you're a lot like me: I work a full-time job, commute two hours a day on public transit, keep a regular exercise schedule, play hockey on three different teams, and have two young children. But I've also managed to write a couple of novels, plot a couple more, and develop this textbook and online course.

To answer the question of where I find the hours to write, let's take a look at my average week.

A lot of people think of their 40-hour work week as taking up most of their time, but the seven days in a week actually clock in at more than four times that length. A week contains 168 hours!

This is how my 168 hours are spent:

- 56 hours of sleep
- 40 hours of work at my day job
- 21 hours of cooking, eating, and cleaning
- 14 hours of taking care of the kids
- 10 hours of commuting to and from work
- 10 hours of weight-lifting, general fitness, and hockey
- 7 hours of dressing, shaving, showering, flossing, and brushing teeth

Add all that up, and I am left with ten hours of free time each week.

Those ten hours are when I write.

Ten hours are enough time for me to get 2,000 finished words written every week. Over eight weeks, I can start 16,000 and get them ready for print; or, in the same eight weeks, excluding revision and polishing, I can finish the entire first draft of a 60,000-word book (about 7,500 words a week, or 750 words an hour), which is what happened with my second novel.

Your own pace probably won't be exactly the same as mine. But you can't find out how fast you work, and how much time you have for writing in a week, until you have consciously, methodically tracked your time. I recommend doing this for seven consecutive days. Don't worry about trying to find seven "typical" days: there's no such thing as a typical day. Just pick a week and track every hour.

There are lots of ways you can do this tracking. Various apps are available, including ecoTouchMedia's *Time Diary*; but people were doing this sort of tracking using pencil and paper long before smartphone apps existed. Do whatever works well for you. More important than the method is the result.

Once you've recorded seven days, identify how your time is spent, and how much time you have available to dedicate to your novel-writing. You can't schedule your writing time properly if you don't know how much time you have to work in the first place.

But what happens if you discover that you really don't have *any* free time? Maybe you're a parent who's up several times a night with a newborn baby. Maybe you're a student taking classes, working a job, and doing mountains of homework on top of it all. What then?

Well, did you notice how much time in my schedule I had dedicated to things like going out for drinks with friends, watching my favourite televisions shows, and going to the movies?

None.

I love doing all those things; but I also know there simply isn't time for them—if I want to achieve my goals and get my books written. As I write this very sentence, I still haven't watched the final season of *Breaking Bad*! It's driving me crazy, and I would love to see how the series concludes; but I've decided that writing this book is more important than watching television.

Are you a *consumer* of art, or a *creator?* The decision has to be made. And, if you choose to be a creator, then you need to keep out of reach of all those time-vacuums, all that junk food we discussed in Step Four. Television, Web-surfing, watching the news—it all has to go.

Laura Vanderkam teaches an excellent CreativeLive course, *Morning Habits of Successful People*, based on her book *What the Most Successful People Do before Breakfast*. Vanderkam is a time-management expert. In interviewing dozens of successful business people, entrepreneurs, and artists, she discovered that almost all of them got up early and did the work that was most important to them before the rest of the world was awake. Before they could be interrupted by children and new email, or distracted by the morning news, they *got the work done.*

It is during those early hours that many people are at their best intellectually and physically. There is a reason why so many of us like to sit on the couch and watch television in the evenings: we're tired! All our energy has been expended. For many people, evenings are not productive time but wasted time; and what successful people consistently do is go to bed early, thereby turning wasted time into sleep-time and the early-morning sleep-time into productive time.

In *The Courage to Write: How Writers Transcend Fear*, Ralph Keyes discusses the habits of several well known authors:

> "   *Trollope thought the key to productivity was being at his desk by 5:30 every morning. Paul Valéry started writing at 5:00 A.M. and seldom wrote past 9:00. Faulkner considered his writing day over by 10:30 or 11:00. For most writers, the morning is a fertile time.*   "

So, if it seems that you have very little free time when you can work uninterrupted, you may want to look into going to bed early, and getting up early, as some of the masters did.

And, of course, there was Benjamin Franklin, who famously repeated the words of John Clarke: "Early to bed and early to rise, makes a man healthy, wealthy, and wise."

If you can't pare anything away *and* it's impossible to get up early, then you'll need to do what I do, which is just write in short bursts, whenever and wherever you can.

Another great book you may want to read is Ariel Gore's *How to Become a Famous Author before You're Dead*. Gore, a single mom, has a great section in her book where she writes about how she keeps a notepad with her at all times and frantically scrawls down sentences whenever she can, even while stopped at red lights in her car! For safety's sake, I can't recommend this tactic; but the point is that, if you want to be writer, you need to write. Whether you admit it or not, you go to the bathroom—probably every day. Right there, sitting on the toilet, you have a few moments when you could do some writing.

Just make it happen.

I use a drafting technique for my manuscripts that requires neither a keyboard nor a pen and paper. I may not always have access to those common writing tools; but, like so many other people, I have a smartphone always within reach.

If I'm struck by a moment of creative inspiration while standing at the bus stop, doing the dishes after dinner, or driving in my car, I simply grab my phone, turn on the voice recorder, and "write" by dictating into the microphone.

I've found this technique especially effective for the early-drafting stage, when simply getting the ideas out is all that really matters. When hands aren't part of the equation, the ideas can flow directly from the brain to the mouth with very little second-guessing; this is a much more direct conduit to the creative unconscious.

When I play back the recording later, there are always lots of "umms" and "uhhs", awkward phrasing, and half-formed ideas, but hidden within that jumbled mess is something I'll be able to work from when I finally have a chance to sit down at a computer and type.

Your smartphone can also be an excellent tool for getting your reading done. We've already discussed how important it is to be a reader, but reading takes a lot of time.

By listening to audio books, you can combine reading with your commute, house-cleaning, and other activities, which may free more time for your writing.

Laura Vanderkam makes another interesting argument about time management. She says that "I don't have the time" really means "It's not a priority." You'll never complete your novel unless you give it a prominent position in the limited time available in your life.

If you are that student or the new parent, writing a novel in this period may not be a realistic option. You have other priorities taking up a good chunk of time. That's life. There is absolutely nothing wrong with remaining in the training stage until you are able to carve out the necessary hours.

There's no point in starting the marathon if you just don't have the time to finish it. Writing a novel is a huge commitment, and your chance of success will be much greater if you're sure you are ready and able to make that commitment.

Homework

Track your time for seven days in a row, and start carving out the time to write.

Challenge 2: Writing a Novel Is an Extremely Lonely Task

HOW TO BEAT IT: There are three solutions for this challenge. You can *embrace the solitary nature of your art form*, you can get *support from a community* of like-minded individuals, and you can remind yourself that *it won't be lonely forever*.

Embrace the Time Alone

We live in an extremely busy world. We're bombarded by the news and entertainment media and by communication technology. Life is already fast, and it's only speeding up. Writing is a wonderful opportunity to get away from all of that. Take up your quill and parchment, and go out into nature. Be like the Lake poets—Wordsworth, Southey, and Coleridge. Get away from the hustle and bustle of the city, the stress of your job, your family, and the digital world. Be at one with nature and yourself, and get some writing done.

Writing is a solitary art form, and that's part of why I love it. It's only really during writing and exercise that all of life's stresses go away and I'm able to feel calm and at one with the world.

If you're a parent, I encourage you to embrace writing as an opportunity for some "me" time. We give so much love, time, and energy to our children that we sometimes forget about our own needs. Writing is about getting lost in other worlds—and it can also be about getting reacquainted with yourself.

Yes, writing a novel requires hours and hours spent alone; but any time alone these days is becoming an increasingly rare commodity. Savour your time alone: it is precious.

Of course, happiness in solitude comes to some people more naturally than to others, and many writers need the energy, support, and feedback of a community. We also must never underestimate the power of human connection.

Seek Community

If loneliness is getting to you, seek community. You're not the only lonely writer—there are lots of them—and there are so many ways you can reach out and connect with them.

Writers' groups exist in almost every community. You can find a group in your neighborhood, or look for city-wide groups organized by local writers' associations. Some groups are specific to certain genres, so seek the one that fits your novel best.

Workshops can be a great way to learn and interact with other writers. This book began as a live workshop, where I taught the material to students in a classroom. As wonderful as reading a book or taking advantage of online learning opportunities can be, the relationships formed with other human beings in person are going to provide you with something that online relationships can never match.

Conventions can be another wonderful way to connect—not only with other writers, but also with agents and publishers in the book industry. Besides exposing you to networks of people who could advance your career in the industry, conventions also are opportunities to discover new books and learn new skills. They're fantastic in so many ways.

Meetup. As of February 2014, the social-networking portal *meetup.com*, which facilitates real-world group gathering, had about sixteen million members in nearly two hundred countries! Meetup groups exist in every major city. Find one near you to interact with other writers, or with readers interested in the same types of books, movies, and hobbies as you. Remember, interacting and community development aren't *just* about connecting with other writers. Forging relationships with artists from diverse media can provide you with entirely new perspectives, and can introduce you to new skills, tools, and systems that you can bring to your own creative process.

With so many different ways to connect in real life, you can't go wrong. If you want community, all you need to do is seek it.

It's not always convenient, however, to leave the house

and meet people at a certain time and place, and not everyone lives where writers' groups are plentiful. For people with those limitations, *the Internet* provides an extremely convenient way to make connections. There is no reason for anyone to feel lonely in the Internet age.

There are *online writers' forums*, where you can participate in discussions, ask your own questions, and answer those from other writers to help them. There also are paid-membership sites, where you can take courses and download unique content and resources—including the Novel Writer's Blueprint site (*yournovelblueprint.com*).

And, of course, there are *social media*. I don't need to list all the different platforms here. You know what they are—and, besides, two years from now, whatever I list in this book may well be outdated.

When it comes to social media, just make sure you are using the proper tool for the job. *Twitter* can be great for sharing links and for contacting people whose work you may want to emulate or from whom you want advice and mentorship. *Facebook* is great for interacting with friends, family, and fans. If your novel is full of images, you probably want to use *Pinterest* or *Tumblr* to promote it. And, if you like making videos, *Vimeo* and *YouTube* are where to connect. Use the right tool for the job.

There are millions of *blogs* out there, many created by writers who would absolutely love for you to visit their sites and comment on their posts. Not only will they appreciate your feedback, but also you can develop relationships with people who are interested in the same topics as you.

In fact, if you haven't already, you probably should start your own blog and begin making connections with potential readers of your novel. The importance of an *author platform* is only increasing. Your platform is the place where new readers can discover you and your work, where you can interact with and tend to your existing fan base, and where you can demonstrate your authority concerning your specific area of expertise. Your platform might be a website, a podcast, a television show, a social-media presence, or some combination. There are now stories about agents and publishers who want to know about an author's platform (such as how many website visitors and Facebook or Twitter followers he or she has) before they're even willing to listen to a pitch for a novel. It is never too early to begin building your audience.

Let's not forget about *family and friends*. More likely than not, these folks are going to be your biggest supporters and your first readers and fans. They can be great when you need moral support, but they can also be some of your most honest critics. I have a close friend who is always willing to take me down a few notches the second my head starts getting too big. At one point, I sent him a concept sketch for the cover of *The Page Turners* that I thought was pretty good. He told me it was generic crap, and pushed me to do better. I went back to work, and came up with the design that my cover artist and I eventually settled on. I might never have gotten to that point if my friend had not been willing to tell me that my original idea wasn't good enough.

Long before anyone else cares about you and your novels, those friends and loved ones are going to be supporting you, so make sure you nourish those relationships.

It Won't Be Lonely Forever

Finally, when it comes to writing and loneliness, remind yourself that it won't be lonely forever.

During the INTRODUCTION to this course, I said that you could produce an ebook with no financial investment whatsoever, but that I didn't recommend it. This is because there are a few areas where you absolutely need to you spend some money in the creation of your book. These three areas are the hiring of a cover artist, an editor, and a designer. After a long, lonely journey, these are the folks you will get to *collaborate* with.

The importance of a striking and professionally designed **book cover** cannot be underestimated. It is tough enough to convince new readers to check out a novel from an indie writer; if you don't have an eye-catching cover that speaks to the professional quality and care that you put in to the production of your book, it's never going to sell. You can write the greatest novel ever, but if you slap a terrible cover on it there's a good chance that no one will discover just what a great work of art you've created. The first impression you give your readers must be top-notch.

As someone who worked as a senior editor on a magazine for several years, I would never publish my writing without first having an *editor* go over it. I view my editor as my partner and an essential part of the creative process of my written products. Editors have a level of expertise that you and I, as fiction writers, will not be able to match. Not every great hockey player makes a great coach, and not every writer has what it takes to edit other people's work. Even if you are decent at editing the words of other writers, your deep and extensive familiarity with your own novel has probably left you blind to certain blemishes that would be obvious to an outsider. You'll want that fresh, outside set of eyes and expertise to help you perfect your book.

Another area that I highly recommend self-published writers invest some cash in is professional *design* for the inside of the book, not just the cover. You can draft a brilliant blueprint and build your house accordingly. But, if, on the inside, the walls are painted fluorescent pink and the furniture doesn't properly fit in the room it's been placed in, all of your inspired architectural design and careful construction will have been a waste. You need the skills of an interior decorator to finish off your home and make it a thing of beauty.

Interior layout and design are something of an invisible art form, and one that you will want to place in the hands of an expert. Bad book design is a lot like obscenity:

people can't always articulate exactly what about it bugs them—but they know it when they see it, even if only subconsciously.

Recto and verso; tracking and kerning; points and picas; widows and orphans; running heads; well designed, coherent typefaces; leading; ligatures; letter- and word-spacing; lining and old-style numerals; line-end hyphenation; em quads; and en rules: these are some of the many things that you may never before have considered, but which are all part of instantly distinguishing a professionally designed book from an amateur effort.

I know you are going to take care to ensure that your intangible prose is as beautiful and elegant as possible. Treat the physical manifestation of your story, the book itself, with the same care: hire a professional designer.

Summary

So, yes, writing is a long, lonely process—but you need to embrace it. If you can't embrace the loneliness, then seek community in real life or online. Finally, don't forget that, at the end of that long road, you get to collaborate with cover artists, editors, and designers, people who are going to take this piece of art that you have put your heart and soul into . . . and make it *even better!* There is a tremendous surge of pride you'll feel when you see the essence of your story, the words, now professionally shaped and packaged, inside and out.

Homework

Identify online and real-life communities and groups to join. If time permits, also get your blog going.

Challenge 3: Writing a Novel Is So Big a Project that It's Intimidating to Start

HOW TO BEAT IT: A *good* start.

You've already been preparing for this throughout THE NOVEL WRITER'S BLUEPRINT. The point of selecting a genre, getting to know its conventions, choosing an established story structure, identifying the big puzzle pieces in your story, attaching those pieces to your structure, and filling in the gaps between them—the point of that entire process—has been to take this vast, complex project, which in theory could be attacked from a hundred different angles, and identify a clear, step-by-step process to follow. I hope that, by now, writing a novel is a much less intimidating project for you.

That said, I do have another solution for you on this one, and that's to make sure you have a good start. When it comes to writing a novel, it's a marathon, not a sprint—but that doesn't mean you can't sprint off the starting-blocks!

In a hockey game, the first five or ten minutes are always pretty frenetic. Players come out flying; but then, normally by the ten-minute mark, things have settled down to the pace and rhythm at which the rest of the game will be played. This is the same thing you want to do with the writing of your novel: come out flying, and then settle in to a reasonable pace that you can maintain steadily for the long term.

My good start to *The Page Turners* happened immediately after grad school. I had just spent a few years surrounded by people who took literature very seriously, and I felt as if I were at an intellectual and personal peak. I had met my wife, who also studied literature; and I had become good friends with my thesis advisor and his wife, who was also a professor of English literature. Since all four of us were writers and academics studying English, I developed this idea that we could all get together for a long weekend, stock up on food, and just write all day long for three solid days. In the evenings, as we ate dinner, we could read to each other what we had written that day and provide comments and encouragement. So that's exactly what we did, and it is how a decent chunk of the first act of my novel was written. It is what gave me the momentum to keep working on the book, draft after draft, year after year.

So make it an event! Don't just say, "Today is the day I start writing my book." Do something special. Go to a cottage for a weekend. Rent a hotel room for a week. Move to Paris for a month if you have the time and money. The point is that, for a limited time, you focus virtually all your energy on the writing of your novel, in order to get that start that will then allow you to settle in to a regular rhythm for the long haul.

You may be familiar already with **National Novel Writing Month**, often called **NaNoWriMo**. Every year, hundreds of thousands of writers each commit to writing a 50,000-word first draft of a novel in November. If you think trying to get it all done in a giant burst might work for you, take a look at *nanowrimo.org* and consider registering to participate next November. Completion rates aren't that great—but you know what? Even the people who fail to reach their goal of 50,000 words that month have a great start to a book, something they can build on in the time that follows.

You'll probably find that those first fifty pages are the most difficult to write, but that once you hit sixty, seventy, or eighty, the ball is really rolling and your writing has become easy.

Well . . . as "easy" as novel-writing gets.

Just make sure you get that great start.

Homework

Decide how you're going to make your start a special event.

Challenge 4: Once You've Started Writing, It's Difficult to Keep Going All the Way to the End

How to beat it: Establish stakes.

Stakes are a pretty simple solution for this problem. Stakes are the consequences for going off track. They keep you accountable and focused on your goals.

In March of 2013, a month after my pneumonia angels appeared to me, I sent four of my closest friends an email. It wasn't long or complicated, but it changed my life forever. The book you're reading right now would not exist if the following email had never been sent:

> " *Hey, guys.*
>
> *By way of this email, I'm committing to completing and publishing my novel by September 2013.*
>
> *Kevin* "

After muddling away on my novel for eight years, I suddenly had a very public deadline, and it was only six months away! I now felt as if I owed it to my friends to live up to my promise and get the book published by that public deadline.

I spent those next six months working as hard as I have ever worked in my life, and, in the end—I missed my deadline. *The Page Turners* wasn't published until the end of November 2013.

But the point isn't that I missed my deadline. The point is that I never would have completed the book *at all* if I hadn't *set* a deadline in the first place, and then created stakes by publicly sharing that deadline with my closest friends.

The publication of that book led me to analyze the job of writing the sequel, which led to the creation of a live workshop to share the system I developed, which led to the creation of the online course and the book you are now reading. All of those things happened because I sent a one-sentence email that established a deadline.

You must not only **create deadlines**, but also implement systems to ensure that you **meet those deadlines**; and public accountability is just one method. Another great tip for establishing stakes, recommended by Tim Ferriss, is the concept of a **reverse charity**. Using this approach, one promises to contribute a certain amount of money to a charitable organization one loathes if one misses a deadline.

A great way to keep up your speed and meet your goals is to **track your progress**. Set daily, weekly, and monthly goals for word counts or parts of the project completed. There are many tools that can help you with this. You can get blog widgets that will list your goal and publicly track your progress towards it. Another technique is to use an old-fashioned wall calendar and a marker. Every day that you meet your daily goal, put a smiley face, gold star sticker, or big green check-mark on that day on your calendar. Inevitably, life will get in the way, you will fall sick, something will come up, and you'll miss your daily goal. When you see that calendar with six days in a row declaring your success, and then that one day with no sticker, it's going to inspire you to get back on track—believe me! And, when you chain together a long string of consecutive days where your goal is met, you can't help but get a sense of accomplishment and progress, which will spur you on further. Clear, visual tracking tools can be extremely helpful.

Mentors and coaches can also be an important resource, not only in teaching and in offering moral support, but also in holding you accountable. Our friends are often overly forgiving when we let them down, and thus aren't always the best source for establishing stakes; generally, letting down a mentor or a parent figure whom you look up to and respect can be a stronger motivator.

If you investigate the habits of successful people, regardless of what field they are in, you'll quickly notice they almost all have mentors, someone who initially showed them the ropes and helped them out, and whose footsteps they followed and modeled. I hope you have someone like that, a coach or a mentor, a friend or a relative, who can offer you that kind of help during your novel-writing. (If you're having trouble finding a mentor, check out the mentorship package offered at the end of this book.)

The End Game

All of this, everything we've talked about over the course of THE NOVEL WRITER'S BLUEPRINT, every single word you've read, note you've taken, and homework assignment you've completed, has been about reaching the end game—having that published book in your hands and in the hands of your readers. There is a lot to juggle, and the many decisions and actions needed to publish a book and sell it can become an easy excuse not to do the hard work of actually writing your book. Your number-one goal, which you should never take your eye off, is YOUR BOOK. If that means you're going to publish your novel and not have a website or blog ready to support it, so be it. If focusing on your book means not going out to the movies for an entire year, then that's what needs to happen. Never forget, everything I have covered in this book is meant to help you write your novel. It's not about social media; it's not about marketing: THE NOVEL WRITER'S BLUEPRINT is about writing your book.

Homework

Set a deadline, and find friends, mentors, and tools to hold yourself accountable.

Conclusion

You've done it! You've made it to the final pages. I am really proud of you for purchasing this book, working your way through the homework assignments, and doing what you need to do to complete your novel and turn your literary dreams into reality.

Look at how far you've come:

- **Step One.** You chose a genre and identified its iconographic and narrative conventions, and used them to pare down your storytelling options to a manageable number.
- **Step Two.** We reviewed the classic story structures that have been successful through time, and you picked the one that appealed to you and used it to structure your narrative.
- **Step Three.** You identified the key puzzle pieces, those big moments that you wanted to get to, or emulate from your favourite works of art; you placed them on your chosen story struc-

CONCLUSION • YOUR FATE = YOUR FATE

ture; and you filled in the gaps between them to develop a beat-sheet.

- **Step Four.** You implemented a preparatory regimen that included a diet of classic literature in general, along with classics and recent bestsellers from your chosen genre, in addition to training exercises to sharpen your writing skills and get your creative juices pumping. And you ensured adequate rest and recovery to support a long, healthy writing career.
- **Step Five.** We discussed the common challenges faced by novelists during the drafting process, and you identified techniques that you'll use to overcome these challenges.

Your FATE = Your Fate

This is the concept with which I want to conclude this book. Todd Henry introduced the idea to me in his CreativeLive course, *Being Creative under Pressure*. Henry also has written a great book, *Die Empty*, which I encourage you to read.

FATE is an acronym for four finite resources that we have in our lives. These are things that we have in *limited* amounts only. We need to be conscious of how we use them, in order to achieve our goals.

Focus. Are you focusing your energy in the right place? Are you putting it into the right aspects of your novel-writing? Is writing a *perfect* first draft really where you should focus your attention, or might simply having a rough but *complete* first draft be a more reasonable goal?

Assets. These are the resources that you have at your disposal to achieve your purpose and get your book written. When you think of assets, cast a wide net—look at many areas of life, including finance, education, technology, and personal relationships. Are you using these assets effectively?

Time. Where you put your time today determines where you will end up tomorrow, and next month, and next year, and even the next decade. If you want that novel in your hands in the near future, you need to dedicate the time to your writing *today*.

Energy. Where your energy goes determines your success or failure. Put your energy into what matters in your life and career. Sending Tweets can be fun and social; but is that the best use of your energy, or would your effort be better directed towards your novel-writing?

Your FATE and your fate are in your hands, so make sure you use these limited resources wisely in creating and finishing your novel.

Farewell

That brings us to the end of THE NOVEL WRITER'S BLUE-PRINT. I've given you my step-by-step program. From here, the rest is up to you.

I wish you all the best.

I believe in you.

Your dreams are about to become reality.

I *know* you can do it.

Now go make it happen.

KEVIN T. JOHNS
Ottawa, Ontario, Canada,
May, 2014.

A Note about Reviews

If you enjoyed this book, it would mean a lot to me if you would take the time to leave a short review on Amazon or Goodreads—or even both!

Reviews help me get this book and program out in front of more struggling writers and first-time authors.

There is no such thing as scarcity when it comes to readers. Fellow authors aren't competitors. A reader of my books is just as likely to be a reader of yours!

The more authors we can all help to achieve their dreams of publishing a book, the more great novels there will be in the world, enriching all of our lives and improving our culture.

And, of course, when you publish YOUR book, please, let me know, so that I can read it and leave a review for you!

Works Cited

All works mentioned in this textbook are listed here, alphabetically within each major part of this text in which they appear.

Preface

Grahl, Tim. *Sell Your First 1000 Books*. CreativeLive course: *creativelive.com / courses / sell-your-first-1000-books-tim-grahl*

———. *Your First 1000 Copies: The Step-by-Step Guide to Marketing Your Book*. Out:think, 2013.

Sumner, Forrest Adam. *brillianteditions.com*

Introduction

Annie Hall. Dir. Woody Allen. 1977.

Brown, Chester. *Paying for It*. Drawn and Quarterly, 2013.

Casablanca. Dir. Michael Curtiz. 1942.

Cobain, Kurt, et al. *In Utero*. Perf. Nirvana. DGC Records, 1993.

Coleridge, Samuel Taylor. *Biographia Literaria; or Biographical Sketches of My Literary Life and Opinions*. 1817.

———. "Kubla Khan". *Christabel, Kubla Khan, and the Pains of Sleep*. 1816.

Darger, Henry Joseph, Jr. *The Story of the Vivian Girls, in What Is Known as the Realms of the Unreal, of the Glandeco–Angelinnian War Storm, Caused by the Child Slave Rebellion.* Unpublished.

Donne, John. *Devotions upon Emergent Occasions, and Severall Steps in My Sicknes.* 1624.

Ellen: The Ellen DeGeneres Show. Host Ellen DeGeneres. Musical guests Tegan and Sara. 13 February 2013: *ellentv.com / videos / 0-0ok4zdzc*

Ferriss, Timothy. *The 4-Hour Chef: The Simple Path to Cooking like a Pro, Learning Anything, and Living the Good Life.* New Harvest, 2012.

Fitzgerald, F. Scott. *The Great Gatsby.* Scribner, 1925.

Hemingway, Ernest. *A Farewell to Arms.* Scribner, 1929.

In the Realms of the Unreal. Dir. Jessica Yu. 2004.

Johns, Kevin T. *The Page Turners: Blood.* Cat & Bean Publishing, 2013.

Kurt Cobain: About a Son. Dir. A. J. Schnack. 2006.

Lawrence of Arabia. Dir. David Lean. 1962.

Mast, Gerald. *A Short History of the Movies.* 3rd ed. University of Chicago Press, 1981. There are also several subsequent editions.

Matt, Joe. *Spent.* Drawn and Quarterly, 2007.

Palahniuk, Chuck. *Fight Club.* W. W. Norton, 1996. This is the source of the mention of Project Mayhem.

Point Break. Dir. Kathryn Bigelow. 1991.

Seth. *It's a Good Life if You Don't Weaken.* Drawn and Quarterly, 2003.

Star Wars. Dir. George Lucas. 1977. Later retitled *Star Wars Episode IV: A New Hope.*

Vonnegut, Kurt, Jr. *Timequake.* Putnam Publishing Group, 1997.

The Wizard of Oz. Dir. Victor Fleming. 1939.

Step One: Genre Selection

Blom, Brendan. "Write On Ottawa: YA Fantasy Novel Offers a Coming-of-Age Gothic Tale". Rev. of *The Page Turners: Blood*, by Kevin T. Johns. *Apt 613*, 23 December 2013: *apt613.ca/write -on-ottawa-the-page-turners*

Brokeback Mountain. Dir. Ang Lee. 2005.

Brooks, Larry. *Story Engineering*. Writer's Digest Books, 2011.

————. *Story Physics: Harnessing the Underlying Forces of Storytelling*. Writer's Digest Books, 2013.

Donne, John. *Devotions upon Emergent Occasions, and Severall Steps in My Sicknes*. 1624.

Dylan, Bob. "Girl from the North Country". Perf. Bob Dylan. *The Freewheelin' Bob Dylan*. 1963.

Firefly. Television series created by Joss Whedon. 2002.

King, Stephen. *'Salem's Lot*. Doubleday, 1975.

"List of Literary Genres". *Wikipedia* (English language). *en.wikipedia.org/wiki/List_of_literary_genres*

McBride, Joseph. *What Ever Happened to Orson Welles?: A Portrait of an Independent Career*. University Press of Kentucky, 2013. On p. 254, Henry Jaglom is quoted as saying, "I was complaining on a particular movie to Orson Welles that I didn't have enough money—that I didn't have enough time—and Orson said to me that 'the enemy of art is the absence of limitations'—that if you had all the time and money in the world to make a movie, then in fact you wouldn't be forced to find creative solutions to problems. If you have money and time, you just throw those things at the problems."

Moore, Christopher. *Bloodsucking Fiends: A Love Story*. Simon & Schuster, 1995.

My Super Ex-Girlfriend. Dir. Ivan Reitman. 2006.

Polidori, John William. "The Vampyre". 1819.

Quick, Matthew. *The Silver Linings Playbook*. Farrar, Straus & Giroux, 2008.

Serenity. Dir. Joss Whedon. 2005.

Shaun of the Dead. Dir. Edgar Wright. 2004.

Silver Linings Playbook. Dir. David O. Russell. 2012.

Stoker, Bram. *Dracula.* 1897.

Step Two: Story Structure

Brooks, Larry. *Story Engineering.* Writer's Digest Books, 2011.

Campbell, Joseph. *The Hero with a Thousand Faces.* Pantheon Books, 1949. There are two more editions: 2nd, 1968; and 3rd, 2008.

Community. Television series created by Dan Harmon. 2009–present.

Dickens, Charles. *A Tale of Two Cities.* 1859.

Donne, John. *Devotions upon Emergent Occasions, and Severall Steps in My Sicknes.* 1624.

Field, Syd. *Screenplay: The Foundations of Screenwriting.* Dell Publishing Company, 1979.

Freytag, Gustav. *Freytag's Technique of the Drama: An Exposition of Dramatic Composition and Art.* 3rd ed. Scott, Foresman and Company, 1894, 1900. Authorized translation, by Elias J. MacEwan, from the 6th German ed. of *Die Technik des Dramas,* of which the 1st ed. was published in 1863.

Harmon, Dan. "Story Structure 101: Super Basic Shit". *Channel 101 Wiki. channel101.wikia.com / wiki / Story_Structure_101:_Super_Basic_Shit*

Holy Bible.

Bell, James Scott. *Build Solid Story Structure & Write Great Fiction.* A *Writer's Digest* tutorial. *tutorials.writersdigest.com / p-417-build-solid-story-structure-write-great-fiction.aspx*

McKree, Robert. *Story: Substance, Structure, Style and the Principles of Screenwriting.* ReganBooks, 1997.

Nixon, Richard Milhous. *RN: The Memoirs of Richard Nixon.* Grosset & Dunlap, 1978.

Propp, Vladimir. *Morphology of the Folktale.* 2nd. ed. revised and edited by Louis A. Wagner, from 1st ed. of translation by Laurence Scott. University of Texas Press, 1968. First Russian-language ed., 1928.

Saramago, José de Sousa. *Blindness.* Translated, 1997, by Giovanni Pontiero, from *Ensaio sobre a cegueira,* 1995.

Star Wars. Dir. George Lucas. 1977. Later retitled *Star Wars Episode IV: A New Hope.*

"Vladimir Propp". *Wikipedia* (English language). *en.wikipedia.org/wiki/Vladimir_Propp* As of the publication date of this book, this is the main Wikipedia article at which to read about Propp's *Morphology of the Folktale.*

The Wizard of Oz. Dir. Victor Fleming. 1939.

Step Three: Puzzle Work

Baum, L. Frank. *The Wonderful Wizard of Oz.* George M. Hill Company, 1900.

Collins, Suzanne. *The Hunger Games.* Scholastic Press, 2008.

The Empire Strikes Back. Dir. Irvin Kershner. 1980. Later retitled *Star Wars Episode V: The Empire Strikes Back.*

Fitzgerald, F. Scott. *The Great Gatsby.* Scribner, 1925.

Johns, Kevin T. *The Page Turners: Blood.* Cat & Bean Publishing, 2013.

Pulp Fiction. Dir. Quentin Tarantino. 1994.

Rowling, J. K. *Harry Potter* book series. 1997–2007.

"Storyteller" (episode 137 of *Buffy the Vampire Slayer*). By Jane Espenson. First broadcast 25 February 2003.

Tolkien, J. R. R. *The Hobbit, or There and Back Again.* George Allen & Unwin, 1937.

————. *The Return of the King.* George Allen & Unwin, 1955.

Woolf, Virginia. *To the Lighthouse.* Hogarth Press, 1927.

"Writing Bytes". *The New York Times Sunday Book Review.* 3 November 2013: BR12. Quoting Rainbow Rowell.

Step Four: Preparatory Regimen

Bradbury, Ray. *The Martian Chronicles*. Doubleday, 1950.

Card, Orson Scott. *Ender's Game*. Tor Books, 1985.

Chandler, Raymond. *The Big Sleep*. Alfred A. Knopf, 1939.

Ferriss, Timothy. *The 4-Hour Body: An Uncommon Guide to Rapid Fat-Loss, Incredible Sex, and Becoming Superhuman*. Harmony, 2010.

———. *The 4-Hour Chef: The Simple Path to Cooking like a Pro, Learning Anything, and Living the Good Life*. New Harvest, 2012.

Fielding, Helen. *Bridget Jones's Diary*. Picador, 1996.

Google Images. Google, Inc. *images.google.com*

Google Maps. Google, Inc. *maps.google.com*

Johns, Kevin T. *The Page Turners: Blood*. Cat & Bean Publishing, 2013.

King, Stephen. *'Salem's Lot*. Doubleday, 1975.

Lewis, C. S. *The Chronicles of Narnia* book series. HarperCollins, 1950–1956.

Steinbeck, John. *The Pastures of Heaven*. Brewer, Warren & Putnam, 1932. An especially good edition is in *John Steinbeck: Novels and Stories, 1932–1937: The Pastures of Heaven / To a God Unknown / Tortilla Flat / In Dubious Battle / Of Mice and Men*, Library of America, 1994.

Tolkien, J. R. R. *The Hobbit, or There and Back Again*. George Allen & Unwin, 1937.

———. *The Lord of the Rings* book series. George Allen & Unwin, 1954–1955.

Wedmore, James. YouTube videos. *youtube.com/user/jameswedmore*

Step Five: Running the Marathon

Breaking Bad. Television series created by Vince Gilligan. 2008–2013.

Clarke, John. *Paroemiologia Anglo-Latina in Usum Scholarum Concinnata, Or, Proverbs English and Latine*. 1639.

ecoTouchMedia. *Time Diary.* iPhone application: *ecotouchmedia.com / apps / apps.html*

Franklin, Benjamin (under pseudonym Richard Saunders). *Poor Richard, 1735: An Almanack for the Year of Christ 1735.* Benjamin Franklin, 1734.

Gore, Ariel. *How to Become a Famous Writer before You're Dead: Your Words in Print and Your Name in Lights.* Three Rivers Press, 2007.

Johns, Kevin T. *The Page Turners: Blood.* Cat & Bean Publishing, 2013.

Keyes, Ralph. *The Courage to Write: How Writers Transcend Fear.* Henry Holt and Company, 1995. Reissue, 2003.

Meetup. *meetup.com*

National Novel Writing Month. *nanowrimo.org*

Vanderkam, Laura. *Morning Habits of Successful People.* CreativeLive course: *creativelive.com / courses / what-most-successful-people-do -breakfast-laura-vanderkam*

———. *What the Most Successful People Do before Breakfast: And Two Other Short Guides to Achieving More at Work and at Home.* Reprint, Portfolio Trade, 2013.

Conclusion

Henry, Todd. *Being Creative under Pressure.* CreativeLive course: *creativelive.com / courses / being-creative-under-pressure-todd-henry*

———. *Die Empty: Unleash Your Best Work Every Day.* Portfolio Hardcover, 2013.

ONE-ON-ONE COACHING OFFER!

I have been lucky enough to have some tremendously helpful teachers and coaches, without whose support I could not have achieved a number of goals in my life, particularly those related to novel-writing.

I would love to play that same role for **you**, and help guide you along **YOUR novel-writing journey**.

To learn more about the **NOVEL WRITER'S BLUEPRINT Mentorship Package**, just email me at kevintjohns@gmail.com with "Mentorship Package" in the subject line.

The Mentorship Package includes a **lifetime membership** to the **NOVEL WRITER'S BLUEPRINT Online Course**, including **all updates and bonus material**!

If you're already a member of the online course, your membership fee will be subtracted from the cost of the Mentorship Package.

Add coupon code EBOOKMENTORSHIPOFFER008 to your email and get **an additional 10% off**!

I look forward to working with you.

Kevin T. Johns
Founder, The Novel Writer's Blueprint

CAT & BEAN PUBLISHING PROUDLY PRESENTS

The *Page Turners* Trilogy

Nate and his friends are thrilled to discover an ancient book of magic spells hidden in the school library — they now have the means to stand up to the villains who make high-school life such a battle. But, when the book's dark magic releases a fictional killer into the real world, the teens will need to prove they have what it takes to be heroes, or fall as bloody victims in their own horror story turned real.

"Kevin T. Johns does a masterful job of making you feel like you're actually there. Highly recommended, this series is on my must-read list."
—SHAWN LACHANCE, *Horror-Writers.net*

"Johns's crimson-stained love letter to genre fiction kept me up late into the night." —BRENDAN BLOM, *Apt613.ca*

"If you like dark tales that don't sugarcoat real-life issues, then this is a great story to pick up." —JULIE DARLEY, *Never Judge a Book by Its Movie*

"The Page Turners *is a shout-out to geeks everywhere. Johns has a voice all his own and does not disappoint. Don't overlook this promising quartet of young heroes."*
—LAUREN SCHARHAG, *Blue House Review*

"I loved it. Five stars for a novel that is fun, scary, and engaging and follows my favourite formula, 'outcast teens take on the world and kick ass'. This book is Freaks and Geeks *meets* Buffy the Vampire Slayer." —CATHERINE BRUNELLE, author of *The Adventures of Claire Never-Ending*

"I enjoyed The Page Turners, *and I'm not usually a young-adult fan. The truest test, however, came when I gave it to my almost thirteen-year-old daughter: she gave it two big thumbs up."*
—BART HOPKINS, *Trueblue Magazine*

Also look for
Books Two and Three
of The *Page Turners* Trilogy.

A prequel chapter to
Book One is available at
thepageturnerstrilogy.com.

Violent bullies. Broken homes. Black magic. Killer fiction.

THE PAGE TURNERS

KEVIN T. JOHNS

Available now, in paperback and ebook, online and in all good bookstores.

NOTES

Notes

THIS BOOK WAS EDITED AND DESIGNED BY
FORREST ADAM SUMNER
BRILLIANTEDITIONS.COM

SINCE 1995

EDITING AND COPYWRITING · COVER DESIGN · INTERIOR DESIGN & LAYOUT
DIAGRAMS, DRAWINGS, GRAPHS, LETTERING, MAPS, AND PHOTOGRAPHS
FROM THE SHORTEST TEXTS TO FULL-LENGTH BOOKS
IN BOTH PRINT AND ELECTRONIC FORMS

STANDARD AND COLLOQUIAL ENGLISH IN NATIONAL VARIETIES
(AMERICAN, BRITISH, CANADIAN, ET CETERA)
CATERING ALSO TO WRITERS FOR WHOM
ENGLISH IS A SECOND LANGUAGE

FICTION AND NONFICTION, PROSE AND VERSE, POPULAR AND LITERARY
ACADEMIC, SCHOLARLY, SCIENTIFIC, AND TECHNICAL
FOR WRITERS AND READERS OF ALL AGES

CPSIA information can be obtained
at www.ICGtesting.com
Printed in the USA
BVHW030341161218
535718BV00001B/350/P